MASTERS AT WORK

# BECOMING
# A FIREFIGHTER

JEFF WILSER

SIMON & SCHUSTER

*New York   London   Toronto   Sydney   New Delhi*

Simon & Schuster
1230 Avenue of the Americas
New York, NY 10020

First Simon & Schuster hardcover edition March 2021

SIMON & SCHUSTER and colophon are registered trademarks
of Simon & Schuster, Inc.

For information about special discounts for bulk purchases,
please contact Simon & Schuster Special Sales at 1-866-506-1949
or business@simonandschuster.com.

The Simon & Schuster Speakers Bureau can bring authors to your
live event. For more information or to book an event, contact the
Simon & Schuster Speakers Bureau at 1-866-248-3049
or visit our website at www.simonspeakers.com.

Illustrations by Donna Mehalko © 2021

Manufactured in the United States of America

1   3   5   7   9   10   8   6   4   2

Library of Congress Cataloging-in-Publication Data

Names: Wilser, Jeff, author.
Title: Becoming a firefighter / Jeff Wilser.
Description: First Simon & Schuster hardcover edition. |
New York : Simon & Schuster, 2021. | Series: Masters at work |
Includes bibliographical references.
Identifiers: LCCN 2020032857 (print) | LCCN 2020032858 (ebook) |
ISBN 9781982139803 (hardcover) | ISBN 9781982139865 (ebook)
Subjects: LCSH: Fire fighters—Missouri—Saint Louis. | Fire
Extinction—Vocational guidance—United States.
Classification: LCC HD8039.F52 U585 2020 (print) |
LCC HD8039.F52 (ebook) | DDC 363.37023/73—dc23
LC record available at https://lccn.loc.gov/2020032857
LC ebook record available at https://lccn.loc.gov/2020032858

ISBN 978-1-9821-3980-3
ISBN 978-1-9821-3986-5 (ebook)

To the past, present, and future
members of the fire service

# CONTENTS

# BECOMING
# A FIREFIGHTER

# INTRODUCTION

We are racing to a child who may die. No one says anything. Ramon slips on white latex gloves. So does Tyler, the firefighter sitting next to him.

It's our ninth run of the day. Five minutes earlier we were joking about chicken wings. The sirens blare. Ramon takes out his phone and checks Active911, an app that syncs to the network of the St. Louis Fire Department (STLFD). *Truck 30: Responding to a child in cardiac arrest.*

As the truck speeds to the scene, Tyler opens the medic bag and grabs the automated external defibrillator (AED). He removes the electrode pads, the ones that send electric shocks to the heart, and replaces them with pediatric pads; if you forget to do this, the normal pads could send too much of a jolt, possibly killing the child.

In less than three minutes we reach the scene, a busy intersection next to a Methodist church. Ramon, Tyler, and their captain fly from the truck and hustle to a small crowd that has gathered over a child. Two ambulances arrived before us—a good sign. I can't see the child because of the crowd.

But I can see the mother.

She's a young woman, African American, and she's crying the sobs of primal anguish. Grief pours from her body. This is a woman who may be watching her daughter die.

The crowd parts as the medics carry out the little girl on a stretcher. She looks to be five years old. Her hair is tied in pigtails. She's motionless, her eyes closed. I can't tell if she is alive or dead.

Now I'm crying. I turn away so the firefighters can't see my tears. The mother shrieks louder. The stretcher is carefully placed inside an ambulance. The back doors close and the ambulance drives away.

On the way to the call, Tyler told me that the odds of saving a child in cardiac arrest were slim, because, realistically, it's tough to get there fast enough to intervene in time.

For a fleeting second the girl flatlined, but the first responders brought her back. They gave her CPR and used the AED and they brought her back.

She was alive. She would live.

This is one of the most wrenching sights I have ever witnessed, but for Ramon and the other firefighters, this is another Tuesday. I would not learn of the girl's fate until later, just as the firefighters, so often, never learn what happens to the people they save, or those they are unable to save. This is just one of the 119,000 calls that the St. Louis

Fire Department responds to every year. This is just one of the 35.3 million calls answered by fire services nationwide.

In most of these 35.3 million calls, the caller is having one of the worst days of their life. They are calling because a teenager has been shot, or their kitchen is in flames, or their boyfriend has overdosed on heroin, or their daughter is in cardiac arrest. They are calling because they need help. They might not even realize that their call to 911 reaches the fire department, but it does. They call for help and they get the help—always, because the fire department never says no. The fire department will help no matter who you are or where you live. Firefighters are wired to help, to serve, to save.

Firefighters do more than fight fire. Today's firefighters are medics, electricians, grief counselors, hazardous material specialists, even defenders of homeland security. They solve problems. They answer prayers. A total of 1.1 million firefighters work together, in small teams, to respond to our nation's emergencies. Around 700,000 of them love the work so much that they do it for free, as volunteer firefighters, while also working nine-to-five jobs.

And then there are the career firefighters. These are the 373,000 men and women who devote their lives—and are willing to sacrifice their lives—to strangers in peril. They worked hard to earn the uniform. They conquered steep odds: some departments are more exclusive than Ivy League schools. And they will likely remain firefighters for the rest of their working lives; in a fluid economy where most of the nation hops from job to job or career to career, firefighters remain firefighters.

Five hundred eighty-seven of these men and women battle fires in St. Louis. It's a proud department, a busy department, a storied department—the second-oldest in the United States, founded in 1857. I spent July of 2019 with this outfit, riding along on calls, sleeping in the bunk rooms, and shadowing firefighters during their twenty-four-hour shifts. For much of America, the concept of a work shift may be outdated, but for firefighters it's foundational. You organize your life by those shifts. In St. Louis the shifts are twenty-four hours on, twenty-four hours off, twenty-four on, twenty-four off, twenty-four on, then four days off. Rinse and repeat.

Given the importance of this twenty-four-hour structure, this book is organized by following one slightly reconstructed twenty-four-hour shift in the St. Louis Fire Department, primarily from the perspectives of three firefighters: Ramon Strickland, twenty-five, a rookie regarded as one of the most respected newbies in the department; Battalion Chief Russ Richter, a thirty-two-year veteran who, according to a survey from *Firehouse* magazine, is the ninth-busiest battalion chief in the nation; and Fire Chief

Dennis Jenkerson, a third-generation firefighter and leader at the top of his field. We'll also hear from firefighters like Captain Mario Montero, a leader of the specialized rescue squad, and Licole McKinney, one of the few female firefighters in the St. Louis Fire Department.

Their stories underscore that when you become a firefighter, you do not just get a new job; you earn an identity. That identity is one of problem-solving, unselfishness, mental toughness, physical strength, versatility, compassion, gallows humor, caregiving, and, above all, service.

Let's start with the new guy.

# I
---
## Morning

## The Prep
6:15 A.M.

Ramon shows up to work early, because Ramon is the new prick. That's what everyone calls him: the new prick. This is not a knock on Ramon. And he's not even that new: he joined the force fifteen months ago. And he's no longer a "probie," a probationary firefighter who's still in their first year. In the fire service, however, tenure is relative. And in the St. Louis Fire Department, it's long-standing tradition to call the greenest firefighter in the firehouse, whether they've been around for two weeks or two years, the new prick.

Like every career firefighter in St. Louis, Ramon has a shift that is twenty-four hours long, from 8:00 a.m. to 8:00 a.m., and he only goes home when the next shift relieves him. Fire-fighters are punctual. Most arrive by 6:30 or 7:00 at the latest or else you're "bum relief." If you show up close to 8:00 a.m., then you're "shit bum relief." The logic? It's a courtesy to the outgoing shift. If you catch a call at, say, 7:45 a.m., then the incoming shift can respond and the outgoing shift won't be stuck at a fire and forced to work late.

"Am I late?" I ask Ramon. It's 6:45 a.m.

He gives me a smile, but he doesn't say no. When I asked to shadow one of the department's most promising rookies, they sent me to Ramon. He's twenty-five, tall, African American, and he wears the most crisply ironed shirt that I will see in my month with the fire department.

"The first thing I do is put my gear on the truck," Ramon tells me, guiding me through the firehouse, one of thirty-two in St. Louis. It's a small building, the way that many actual firehouses are smaller than you would expect: a garage just roomy enough for the one fire truck; a small den with a couple of bachelor pad–looking easy chairs that face a TV; an upstairs with lockers and showers; a tiny weight room; and open sleeping quarters with twin-size beds that stand upright during the day. There are only four firefighters here at any one point in time. (Some larger departments, such as Chicago or Los Angeles, have the kind of multi-company, crowded, and rowdy firefighter stations that you see on TV, but many of the nation's 50,000 firehouses look more like this.)

The fire truck, of course, is the star of the station. It's thirty feet long and gleaming red, and it looks like a bull about to charge. An extendable white ladder rests along the spine of the truck and hangs over the front of the cab. Ramon inspects all of the gear on the truck, the gear in his locker, the gear on his body. He triple-checks the self-contained breathing apparatus (SCBA), aka the oxygen mask, aka "the mask." The SCBA is to a firefighter what the rifle is to a marine. Introduced in the 1970s and fully embraced in the 1990s, the mask, along with the flame-resistant turnout gear, allows firefighters to work in previously unworkable conditions. This lets them aggressively attack the "seat of the fire," or the point of origin.

"You hear this beeping?" Ramon asks. First a quiet beep,

then a louder *beep*, then a *BEEP! BEEP!* It's a piercing sound that stabs your ears. Ramon explains that the SCBA has a variety of safety gizmos like this beep, which is activated if it detects that a firefighter is not moving, and possibly unconscious. Every day he checks them all.

Ramon inspects the bunker gear, also called turnout gear. A chalky dark gray with yellow reflecting strips, these workhorse field uniforms are made of thick Nomex, a rubbery material that's sometimes used to make space suits and that lets you walk through fire. As an Illinois-based fire chief told me, here's what it's like to wear the bunker gear: "Put on your warmest winter clothing, like a snowsuit. And then put another layer on top of that. Then get on a treadmill and run as fast as you can. And now I'm going to spray you with hot water and throw rocks at you."

Ramon's shift has officially begun. The next call will be answered by Ramon and the rest of Truck 30's four-firefighter crew. But first, morning chores. Today is a Tuesday, and Tuesday is L day: lawns, lockers, and ladders. Ramon needs to cut the grass, deep-clean the lockers, and do a closer inspection of all the ladders: the twelve-footer, the twenty-four-footer, and the thirty-five-footer atop the truck.

"What's next?" I ask him.

"I'm going to scrub the toilets," he says, glancing at my journal. "You want to take notes on this?"

9:00 A.M.

While the rookies scrub the commodes, the senior officers scrub the paperwork. On the first floor of the STLFD head-quarters, a two-story building that looks a bit like an elementary school, is a small office filled with large men. This is the daily command staff meeting. Ramon's boss is a fire captain. And the captains report to the battalion chiefs, who now gather in this office to assemble the daily roster of who, exactly, will fight the city's fires.

At one end of the table is Battalion Chief Russ Richter, who stands an imposing six feet five inches, with a buzz cut, red face, and handlebar mustache. In Richter's own words, he's "Hoosier strong": not the kind of chiseled physique you see on a sexy firemen calendar, but the kind of man who looks like he could throw a refrigerator. His uniform includes a fire department radio, Buck knife, and Chuck Norris pin. He's in charge of the A Shift (there are three shifts total) of the Fifth District (there are six districts total), the busiest in St. Louis. In 2018, Richter had 2,890 runs. The department's public information officer, Captain Garon Mosby, calls Richter the "most tactically brilliant firefighter in the city."

Richter is seated at the table, hunched over his paperwork. He lugs around a binder four inches thick, like a Trapper

Keeper for grown-ups, impeccably organized with high-lighters and pencils and erasers. The paperwork is done by hand. Looking up from the binder, he tells me in his deep, gravelly voice, "It's 2019, and I'm using a fucking pencil."

The binder contains the manpower logs for each of his four fire stations, and, yes, they still use the word "manpower," just as many firefighters still slip and say "firemen." (There are more mustaches in the St. Louis Fire Department than there are women: fifteen female firefighters out of 587, or 2.6 percent, roughly in line with the anemic national average of 4 percent.)

Every morning the battalion chiefs review the manpower sheets like accountants to ensure that the department is fully operational. Botched paperwork can botch a fire.

"People are always calling in sick," one of the chiefs tells me, leaning back in his chair. The old-timers in the room complain that, unlike in their generation, millennial fire-fighters are more likely to call in sick. With every canceled shift, the chiefs must rejigger the schedule by calling in fire-fighters on their off days; most are eager to volunteer for the plum overtime. This is the kind of unseen work required to keep the ball spinning, nationwide, for a round-the-clock, 1.1-million-person network that can never fail.

Richter looks up from the binder. Done. Then he shoots me a look that says, *Let's get the fuck out of here.* The second we leave the building he lights a cigarette, one of the approximately 15,000 cigarettes he will smoke over the next twenty-four hours. I ask him if smoking is even allowed.

"The rules say that the officer can designate the smoking area," Richter tells me. "So, wherever I am, that's the smoking area."

HANGING ON THE WALL of Ramon's station house is a framed photograph of an old-timey fire chief, a portrait that's so classically heroic-midwestern firefighter—stern eyes, thick mustache, hard and handsome face—that it almost looks fake. This is a portrait of Dennis Jenkerson, the current fire chief of St. Louis. And his morning's prep work begins even earlier than Ramon's or Richter's.

It's only a bit of a stretch to say that the fire chief never sleeps. Next to his pillow stands his phone, a backup phone, and a fire department radio. He wants to hear everything. Like the CEO of a large company, Jenkerson is responsible for a sprawling organization that includes a $62 million budget, seven hundred employees, thirty-two fire stations, and a fleet of trucks and pumpers and hook and ladders. Unlike a CEO, if he makes a poor decision, his employees could die. So he listens. Every night, using an earpiece to avoid waking his wife, he monitors the status of any active fires, listening to the captain on the scene. He's been doing this long enough that he can tell, just from the inflection of the captain's voice, whether he needs to take action.

At 5:15 a.m. he wakes up for good. Something's bothering him: he needs more medics. St. Louis has the highest per capita murder rate in the nation. (More than one Uber driver mentioned this fact to me, almost as a point of civic pride. As one driver put it, "Everyone talks about Baltimore, but things here are bad.")

Shootings happen daily. And Jenkerson knows there's a link between gun violence and calls to the fire department, just as there's a link between almost everything and calls to the fire department. A summer heat wave? Then a spike in emergency medical services (EMS) calls, because of heat-strokes. Construction of a new high-rise building? That could disrupt the routes of his ambulances. The Cardinals force Game 6 in a playoff series? Then he needs to staff Busch Stadium with a fire watch. This is why every morning at 5:30 a.m., over two cups of coffee, Jenkerson reads the *St. Louis Post-Dispatch* from cover to cover, then the *St. Louis Business Journal* from cover to cover, then the *St. Louis/Southern Illinois Labor Tribune*, and then he skims the *Wall Street Journal* while listening to the local news in the background. A fire chief must be a news junkie.

Since Jenkerson took the reins in 2007, civilian fire deaths in St. Louis have all but disappeared; they're in the single digits each year. When a home insurance website released a ranking of the most fire-safe cities in the Midwest, they crowned St. Louis as number one. The city no longer burns, but it still bleeds. Sixty-one percent of the calls to the fire department are for medical runs; nationwide it's 64 percent.

When fully staffed, his department should have fifty-five paramedics. Now he's twenty medics short—40 percent below his target—thanks, in part, to the city's shootings. Every time someone in St. Louis gets shot, firefighters or paramedics race to the scene. Eighty-five percent of the time, Jenkerson estimates, they get there fast enough to stanch the bleeding and save the victim's life. His department includes 587 firefighters and 130 EMS responders, including the paramedics. Nearly all firefighters are cross-trained in emergency medical services, but a shortage of paramedics adds pressure to the firefighters. Days earlier, in a local radio interview, Jenkerson said that paramedics are "quitting faster than I can replace them," explaining that, because of the high crime rate, paramedics are seeing "a lot of bloodshed. And when you get into the bloodshed that involves children, it gets to you."

The solution? Give the medics a pay bump and hire more, which would lighten the load. But that's not easy to do. Thanks to bureaucratic red tape, all personnel decisions must be approved by the mayor's office, and so far the politicians haven't helped. So Jenkerson gave the radio journalist a juicy sound bite: "These are paramedics, not combat medics."

That line was a bit of a political gamble. Jenkerson's boss's boss is the mayor of St. Louis. Likening the paramedics to combat medics implied that the city was in a war zone, which could be seen as a swipe at the mayor. The line was so inflammatory that the department's head of communications, Captain Mosby, cautioned the chief about blowback: Was Jenkerson sure he wanted to go there?

Jenkerson knew what he was doing. The bureaucracy, in his view, was not getting it done. Maybe he could use the press to nudge popular opinion, putting heat on the politicians. Hours after the radio spot ran, Firehouse.com picked up the story and used the headline "St. Louis Paramedics Quit over 'Bloodshed.'" Two local news stations immediately booked him for TV interviews.

I watch as Jenkerson gives the TV interviews in his office, from behind an imposing wooden desk, flanked by an American flag and the red St. Louis city flag. It's a good look. Jenkerson is sixty-two, tall, trim, with a soldier's posture. It takes a certain confidence to wear his bold salt-and-pepper mustache, which looks like a throwback to the Civil War.

The camera guy sets up the shot. Jenkerson chats with the news reporter, a young woman in a purple dress. He knows the reporter and they swap jokes about barbecues and the St. Louis Fair. He clips on his mic like a pro; he's good at this.

The camera flicks on. Everyone is all business. "This is pretty concerning," the reporter says in her reporter voice. "What's happening with paramedics here?"

Jenkerson sticks to his talking points. Not only is he twenty paramedics short, but there aren't even any applicants. "We have nobody left to interview," he says. "We're seeing the effect of some of the trauma in the city. It's starting to take a toll on our men and women who want to be EMTs and paramedics."

When asked, the chief clarifies the difference: EMTs are trained medical first responders, but, unlike paramedics, they are not allowed to administer drugs. Every firefighter is required to get certified as an EMT, and many are also trained as paramedics. And all of them are seeing more trauma. "You can't continually see people thrown from automobiles, and injuries to small children, without it taking a toll," he says.

"Am I at risk?" the reporter asks.

"You're not at risk," the chief coolly reassures her, adding that he can make things work—for now—with the Band-Aid of extra overtime for firefighters. Left unspoken is this fundamental truth: firefighters are the ones picking up the slack. This is what they do.

As soon as the interview ends, a second TV crew enters

and Jenkerson repeats the performance, just as smoothly, with a pitch-perfect mix of gravitas, reassurance, and calming humor.

Later, after the TV spots air, the fire chief swings by the office of Garon Mosby, the public information officer, a cheerful forty-two-year-old African American man who sometimes calls one of the deputy chiefs "Lord Commander," as a nod to *Game of Thrones*. (Mosby has since become something of a budding TV personality, providing commentary on A&E's *Live Rescue*, a reality show that follows the St. Louis Fire Department.)

"It's already started," Jenkerson says. With a knowing smile, he holds up his phone and shows Mosby a tweet: someone linked to the interview and tweeted that the mayor had "blood on her hands."

Technically they slightly misquoted the fire chief, but the message has been sent.

## Cutting Grass, Cutting Teeth

9:15 A.M.

The July morning is already baking hot. Ramon has hopped on the lawn mower and is cutting the grass, something he can do in his sleep. In a sense, cutting grass is part of how he became a firefighter.

Ramon does not come from a firefighting family. His father passed away when he was two; his mom worked for the St. Louis Forestry Division. He has wanted to be a firefighter since he was a kid, but he knew it would take a ton of time, hard work, and luck. "Getting hired on a fire department anywhere in the United States is incredibly, incredibly competitive," says Captain Jason Brezler of the New York City Fire Department (FDNY). He points out that in New York, for example, every year, more than 40,000 people apply to be firefighters. Only a few thousand are hired, meaning 90 percent are not. As Brezler notes, "The numbers are on par with Ivy League institutions."

Becoming a firefighter—specifically a salaried career firefighter, the scope of this book—can be a long, frustrating, and confusing journey. For starters, you may not know when they're hiring, or even *if* they're hiring. Here's how it works in St. Louis. Once every few years—maybe three, maybe five, depending on their hiring needs—the city will announce a test. The test has two components: written and physical. If you pass the test—every year the cutoff score is different— then you're put on a list of potential recruits.

In early 2016, Ramon prepared to take the St. Louis firefighter's test. Some firefighters say that the written test is "not a big deal," simply a basic evaluation of reading comprehension and math. Ramon viewed it differently. He studied three hours a day for five months, drilling himself with practice exams. He also trained for the physical test. Unlike the military, which tests you with a mix of sit-ups, pull-ups, and a timed run, the firefighter's exam runs you through the sweaty tasks you will actually do as a firefighter: toss ladders, haul the hose, swing an ax. You pound a tire with a sledgehammer as many times as you can, as in the kind of event you'd see on ESPN 7. So again Ramon trained. Even though he was already in peak physical condition—in high school he played quarterback, tossing twelve touchdown passes and rushing for another eleven—he spent two months simulating firefighting drills, *Rocky*-training-montage style.

While the test is theoretically just those two components, written and physical, which you combine for a total score, the reality is that, in most city departments, you can boost your score with bonus points: points for having an EMS license, points for military service, points if you work in the city government. Many departments give you points if you have a firefighter in your family, which helps explain why there are so many legacy firefighters.

The points are a big deal. If you tested slightly better than your buddy but he has an EMS license and you don't, there's a good chance he'll jump you on the list. Many aspiring firefighters do everything they can to max out these bonus points, such as first getting certified as an EMS or even getting a job with the city. There's no national standard. Like so much of the fire service, the exact guidelines are case by case. (As Chief Billy Goldfeder, author of the *Pass It On* series of fire service leadership books, once told me, "If you've seen one fire department, you've seen one fire department.")

In New York, for example, you get 5 additional points if you're a veteran, 5 if you're a city resident, and 10 if your father was a firefighter killed in the line of duty. FDNY's Brezler says that if you live on Long Island, and you're not a city resident and you're not a military vet, then even if you crush the test, "the chances of you getting hired are very, very, very slim." And the Chicago Fire Department, by contrast, is a de facto lottery. You take the test and it's pass or fail, and if you pass you're thrown into a pool, and then they pluck names from that pool using random Social Security numbers.

"They're all different," another fire chief told me. "It's so locally driven, and it's politically driven. When the politics changes, the testing changes." The best strategy, no matter where you live: Go to a local firehouse and ask them how it works. Firefighters are eager to help other firefighters and would-be firefighters.

Ramon knew about the bonus points. So, with an eye toward the ultimate prize of becoming a firefighter, he landed a city job cutting grass for the St. Louis parks department. He then moved to the forestry division, where he chopped down trees. And after all of this preparation, in the summer of 2016, Ramon took the test with around 3,000 other hopefuls. About five hundred people "passed," but it's unlikely that all five hundred will become firefighters—at least, not anytime soon. Ramon landed on the list at number ninety-three, or in the top 3 percent of all applicants, but even that wasn't a guarantee.

The second wrinkle in the process: timing.

When you're on the list, the only thing that means is that your number could be called when, and if, the department has openings. The number of openings can change. After Ramon took the test—and nailed it—he went back to chopping down trees, waiting for an acceptance letter that might never arrive. The months ticked by. Then, in March of 2017, good news: the St. Louis Fire Department announced that they would open a class of fifty firefighters. At the time Ramon thought, *Cool. Each time they'll do classes of fifty, and I'm number ninety-three, so the next time I'll make it.* (Most of the first fifty on the list had prior military experience, underscoring the importance of those bonus points.) With those fifty off the board, now Ramon moved up to number forty-three.

A few months later they announced another class: forty-two people. Ramon had missed it by one slot.

Now he was number one on the list.

Another six months rolled by; no more openings. Ramon

cut more grass, chopped down more trees. More months ticked by; no more openings.

The worst part? When the fire department decides to do another test, the old list is scotched. You start over. This means that every morning when Ramon went to go chop trees, there was a chance that either (a) his number would get called, or (b) the list would go up in smoke. The specifics vary, but Ramon's experience is not uncommon. This agonizing waiting game is one reason why, as Fire Chief Tom Jenkins of Rogers, Arkansas, told me, "everyone who's in the service realizes that for every one who made it, there are ninety-nine who didn't." Another told me that getting hired feels like winning the lottery.

Ramon had taken the test in the summer of 2016. Nearly eighteen months later he opened his mailbox to find that coveted letter: his number had come up.

Game on.

At last he would attend the St. Louis Fire Academy, an intense twelve-week program that begins every day at 6:30 a.m., sharp, with an hour of PT. "It was brutal," he recalls, calling it "ten times worse than football practice." Every morning they did the "ten tens": ten sit-ups (easy), ten burpees (no sweat), and then sprinting up the stairs of the six-story training tower that looms in the parking lot of the STLFD headquarters (harder). Then you do it again. And again. You are supposed to do it ten times. Ramon, the former quarterback who appears to have less than 5 percent body fat, couldn't finish the drill; he only made it to eight. By the end of the academy he would get to ten.

After PT there was no time to shower. By 8:00 a.m. Ramon was in his uniform of red polo shirt, navy pants, and black boots that he had shined to a liquid black. Then they hit the classroom to study a dense 1,372-page textbook, *Essentials of Fire Fighting*, a bible of technical details like how class A foam differs from class B foam, as the latter "may be used with fog nozzles, air-aspirating foam nozzles, medium- and high-expansion devices, and compressed air foam systems (CAFS)" and is effective on "petroleum-based combustible or flammable liquids that float on water including: crude oil, fuel oil, gasoline, benzene, naphtha, jet fuel, kerosene," and you get the idea. Firefighters memorize all of this. They get it down cold. Yes, firefighters are brave. Everybody knows that firefighters are brave. What's less understood is that a good firefighter must be an exceptional student, and it's an act of bravery just to read that goddamn 1,372-page book.

More studying. Then a quick lunch. Then an afternoon packed with drill after drill: tying knots, throwing ladders, hoisting power saws, rappelling down the side of a building, removing car windshields, cutting ventilation holes in roofs, sizing up a scene, learning the crucial difference between an offensive attack (an interior strike at the seat of the fire) and a defensive stand (spraying water from a safe distance), and the other core elements of firefighting.

Little of it is straightforward. Nuance abounds. Ventilation, for example, is a complex subject and can be a tricky problem even for veteran firefighters. "The trench cut," *Essentials of Fire Fighting* explains, "is strictly a defensive operation and should NOT be confused with or used as offensive vertical ventilation. Offensive vertical ventilation techniques are used primarily to remove heat, smoke, and gases from the structure and are best done directly above the fire." It goes on like this for quite some time. Like a lawyer studying the intricacies of tort law, a firefighter needs to master the arcana. Unlike a lawyer, if you don't study hard enough, you might die.

Around 5:00 p.m., when much of the nation finishes work and cracks a beer, the aspiring firefighters do a second round of PT. Ramon and his twenty-two classmates get dressed in full bunker gear, do push-ups, and once again race up the training tower. The bunker gear and the SCBA weigh forty-five pounds. They run up that tower a second time, a third time, a seventh time. They do it until they're ready to puke.

Jenkerson prides himself on training the hell out of his firefighters. They teach the basics of "Firefighter I" and "Firefighter II" (the standards set by the National Fire Protection Association, or NFPA), but then they go further. "I'll talk to new recruits who are so tired of tying knots and lifting ladders," he says. His goal is not to train them until they get it right. His goal is to train them so hard, and to give them so many reps, that the skill is deeply ingrained in their muscle memory and they will "never, ever get it wrong." You don't stop training the moment you learn how to tie a clove hitch. You stop training only when you can tie a clove hitch at the bottom of an elevator shaft, in the dark, without breathing.

Another purpose of the academy, says Jenkerson, is to instill the values of a paramilitary organization. Fires don't afford time for "please" and "thank you." "It's rough and straightforward and can seem rude," says the fire chief. "A lot of what we do at the academy is to make sure recruits understand this." Like United States Marine Corps boot camp, the training is designed to build teamwork, and it does that with tough love. If a recruit has forgotten their belt on the way to class, then everyone does push-ups until the recruit returns with the belt. "All of the sudden guys start carrying extra belts in their locker, just in case they need to help someone out," Jenkerson says.

Finally, at the end of each day of the academy, Ramon would get home, cook a quick dinner, wash his uniform, shine his boots, and then begin studying at 8:00 p.m.

"Wait, more studying?" I ask him. "Really?"

"I had to."

"How long?"

"I studied until midnight," he says. "I'm not a first-time getter. It takes me a couple of times to see the material, so I need to study."

Then, at midnight, he arranged his gear by the end of his bed so he could grab it at 5:00 in the morning and do it all over again.

IF RAMON'S PATH GIVES a glimpse of how to break into the ranks of firefighters, Jenkerson's provides a look at how to ascend to the rank of fire chief.

Jenkerson's father was a firefighter. His grandfather was a firefighter. A tough Irishman, his grandfather joined the fire service in the Great Depression. Back then the battalion chiefs wore white rubber coats, white metal helmets, and no goggles or breathing masks. "He was this great, burly chested, hairy guy. He looked like a superhero," says Jenkerson, remembering that his grandfather clung to the back of the moving fire truck, the way firemen used to do. His grandfather used to take him to a firemen's bar and let him sip on a penny Coke.

One day his grandfather fought a fire in a drugstore. A boiler in the basement had exploded. Decades before the

SCBA, his grandfather inhaled the hot gases and blistered his lungs. He burned his hands. He went back to work the next day, but he was in too much pain and got sent home. When Dennis was just seven years old, he watched as his grandfather struggled to open a bottle of Busch with his bandaged hands. He watched his grandfather lying on the floor, in agony, from his burned lungs. And then, weeks later, he watched as his grandfather was given the honors of a fireman's funeral.

Later, as a teenager, Dennis saw the toll that firefighting took on his father. "I would see my father come home tired, dirty, stinky, trying to get an hour of sleep on the living room floor," he tells me. He saw the injuries to his father mount: broken hips, busted ribs, cut hands. *No way*, he said to himself. *I'm not doing this.*

In what might have been a low-key rebellion, Jenkerson went to Missouri Southern College on a soccer scholarship, and thought he would become a dentist. Yet the childhood dream lingered, as it so often does for the sons of firefighters. When the fire department offered a test in 1978, almost on a lark, Jenkerson took the test along with more than a thousand other people. Jenkerson finished in the top ten. He interviewed with the fire chief, who asked him, "Why do you want this job?"

"I'm not sure I do," he answered.

Yet, in the end, of course, he did. Over the years he's sensed that being a firefighter isn't a job; it's an identity. Most consider it a calling. "As I grew up, everyone told me that 'your grandfather was one hell of a man,'" he says, and he began to realize that something set his grandfather apart from the grandfathers of his friends.

Jenkerson enrolled in the St. Louis Fire Academy in 1979. And then the instructors did everything they could to do one simple thing: make him fail. "You're not your father. You're not your grandfather. You're nothing. You ain't never going to be like your daddy!" one instructor, an ex–Green Beret, barked at him. He was hazed. Jenkerson knew that if he fumbled or failed, the stories would get back to his father. He felt the pressure to do better than everybody else.

So he did. When he graduated the academy, as a new prick, he studied every night. And he did this for the next forty years. He adopted the study habits of his father, who read technical manuals for an hour each evening, no matter how tired. He recommends this habit to all firefighters. "Even if you retain only one page out of every fifty," Jenkerson says, "you're still ahead of everybody else." In preparation for the captain's exam, he studied hours every night for months.

You have to study for the captain's test. It's one of the most stressful exams in the United States. If you flub the SAT, you can redeem yourself on the next one. If you're a lawyer who fails the bar, you can take a mulligan. But if you fail the captain's exam, you might not get a chance for another five or seven years: just like the test to join the fire department, it's offered only occasionally.

That year roughly four hundred firefighters took the captain's exam. Jenkerson had the third-highest score. That same year his father, then a deputy chief, took the fire chief's exam. Two other deputies also took the test. His father finished with the highest score, but wasn't chosen.

Jenkerson was pissed on his father's behalf. "It was politics," he tells me now. At the time he confronted the local politicians and told them, "You've just made the biggest mistake of your political career."

Disgusted with what felt like a broken system, Jenkerson thought about quitting. In a bit of insult to injury, the new fire chief—the one chosen over his father—transferred him to one of the glummest assignments in the city: the fire station at Lambert–St. Louis International Airport, which was isolated from most of the city's action. This was basically that scene in every cop movie where the captain warns the maverick hero, "You'll be stuck writing traffic tickets."

Jenkerson didn't quit. Instead, he channeled that anger into something close to avenging his father: *I'm going to get that top job.* If he was stuck at the airport? Fine. He would use the downtime to load up on classes: aircraft rescue training, hazmat training, military ejection seat training.

He paid for some courses out of his own pocket. In what little free time he had, he took college courses and now holds degrees in both fire engineering and organizational leadership, loading up on classes in biology and psychology. He graduated from Saint Louis University, summa cum laude, and deepened his knowledge in accounting, statistics, and philosophy. (Jenkerson regularly refers to Maslow's hierarchy of needs. With enthusiasm he showed me his old psychology textbooks, which are extensively underlined and the margins filled with notes.)

In fact, Jenkerson studied so hard for the battalion chief's exam that he thought he would get divorced over it. (He wouldn't. He's been married to his wife for forty years.) And he began prepping for the fire chief's exam the day he was promoted to battalion chief. "It was a ten-year strategy," he says.

The plan: Jenkerson saw from his own father that, to become fire chief, being an extraordinary firefighter is not enough. And studying your ass off is not enough. You need to know people. You need to play the game. So he made it a mission to embed himself in the local community. He took leadership roles in nonprofit organizations with high visibility, like the St. Louis Fair, Guns 'N Hoses (a charity boxing event for police and firefighters), marathon runs, and Back-Stoppers, the organization that provides for the families of fallen firefighters. Most of these positions were unpaid. He wanted to be known as the guy for any large community event, so if a civic leader asked, "Hey, we're going to launch fifty hot-air balloons in Forest Park. Who should we call for fire protection?" the answer was Dennis Jenkerson.

He didn't stop there. Jenkerson sensed that local leaders had political ambitions well beyond St. Louis, so he made connections in Washington, D.C., joining antiterrorism boards with the Department of Homeland Security and also the Metropolitan Medical Response System. Soon his Rolodex became as impeccable as his résumé. Between his official role as battalion chief and all of the volunteering and networking— plus a side gig as a carpenter (almost every firefighter has a side gig)—he worked one hundred hours per week.

By the time he was up for the fire chief's exam, in 2007, he knew that his credentials were bulletproof. He was the battalion chief for the busiest district of the city: the Fifth, the same as Richter today. He had experience in every district of the city, including the airport. He had technical degrees up the wazoo. He had put in the community work.

Yet he didn't stop there. The fire chief's exam isn't really an exam. It's a multiday, marathon, unstructured interview with a panel of civic leaders. He didn't wing it. Jenkerson never wings it. He scripted a detailed presentation that outlined his vision for the fire department. He memorized the speech. Then he recorded himself and listened to the playback on his iPod while driving to work, finding ways to tweak the language. Then he recorded the revised speech and listened to it again on his iPod. Made more changes. Asked others to listen to the speech. Asked himself, *Am I being inclusive enough? Am I getting enough diverse points of view?* He asked an African American woman in charge of the nursing department for input: "How does this sound to you?" He listened to it in the basement when lifting weights. (At 6:30 every morning Jenkerson lifts weights, and in between sets he jots down notes for the day's priorities on index cards, which he keeps in his breast pocket.) He practiced the speech with his wife. "I listened to that speech probably one hundred times," he says. He wanted the presentation to be so fucking good that it would be impossible for them to say no.

He was fifty years old, one of the youngest fire chiefs in the department's history, when they said yes.

## New Construction, New Dangers

10:00 A.M.

After Richter knocks out his paperwork, we hop in his red SUV, which, like every vehicle in the fire department, is tricked out with a computer showing the city's map, active calls, and locations of the trucks and pumpers and hook and ladders. Last night, when Richter was off duty, his district caught some fires, so he wants to inspect the burned buildings to see what happened and, perhaps, learn what could have been done differently.

Richter's district cuts through the city's haves and have-nots. There seem to be more of the latter. "I've got the richest and the poorest people in the city," Richter tells me from the driver's seat. A century ago, with a population of 575,000, St. Louis was the fourth-largest city in the nation. It hosted the 1904 World's Fair. The treasures of the Gateway City would include music (from Chuck Berry to Miles Davis), literature (from T. S. Eliot to Maya Angelou), commerce (from Anheuser-Busch to a booming advertising industry), and sports (Yogi Berra is a hometown hero).

That was then. St. Louis shrinks while the nation expands; with a population of 303,000 (5 percent lower than the last census), it is now the sixty-fourth largest city in the United States, or two spots beneath Henderson, Nevada. Yet, as the novelist Jane Smiley suggests in a 2019 piece for the *New York Times*, St. Louis is "perhaps the most enlightening spot in America for exploring what America really is."

Swanky neighborhoods like the Central West End— teeming with cafés and Whole Foods and high-rise condos (one is optimistically called "the Tribeca")—are only blocks away from a grim stretch of abandoned buildings, empty lots, and homeless encampments. There are 7,000 vacant buildings in St. Louis. The bulk of the shootings happen in these neighborhoods. On a chalkboard by one of these buildings, someone wrote in large block letters: *How many kids have to die before enough is enough?*

As we drive through these bleak neighborhoods, Richter points out the many buildings that were once on fire. "That one burned down." Across the street: "That one was a house fire." A block later: "There's another." Every block has a story. For over thirty years he has battled fires in the husks of these buildings, sometimes saving lives, sometimes finding bodies. Sometimes he's called back to the same building he once saved and watches it burn all over again.

He points to another abandoned house. In that fire they found an unconscious dog, a white terrier. "We tried to revive the dog with CPR," he says in his deep, gruff voice. "The dog died. It was sad. Nobody wants to see a dog die. He didn't do anything wrong." He pauses. "It's sad when anything dies." We drive for a bit longer in silence, and he looks at me and says, "This is the saddest tour in the history of tours."

We pass more abandoned buildings. The chief sees two men, both African American, sitting on a stoop. Richter waves to them. The men wave back with a look of recognition.

"How do you know them?"

"I put out a fire in the building next to them." He shrugs. "Saved their house."

The risk of fire is not borne equally by society. Poor neighborhoods burn. "Rich people tend not to burn their own property," says Richter. This doesn't mean that impoverished people are committing arson, he clarifies, but that they're more likely to have accidents. With fewer options for entertainment, they're more likely to play in abandoned buildings. Or a homeless squatter might, say, heat a can of soup over an open flame. So these vacant buildings are a fire hazard, especially in the winter, when the open flames are used for warmth. Richter wants to see them torn down. But that costs money, and since a shrinking population translates to a drop in tax revenue, the city's coffers suffer.

In the low-income neighborhood of Hamilton Heights, Richter pulls up to a house that caught afire last night. He lights a cigarette.

We step inside the two-story home. The bottom floor is unscathed, but the top floor is demolished. The drywall has crumbled. Soggy tufts of insulation spill from the wooden beams, like cotton candy in a dumpster. The roof has a hole in it where the firefighters cut a square to ventilate the smoke and heat. The floor is coated with layers of ash and dirt and gunk; my white sneakers turn black. There's no furniture, no TV, no books or clothes or toys—no sign that a low-income family lived in this room just twenty-four hours earlier.

The chief points to some black streaks on the walls of the stairwell. "That's where they came in," he says, meaning the firefighters. "Those are the hand marks." He's like an ace detective examining the crime scene. And he's curious about where the fire started. He combs through the wreckage and makes his way to a bedroom, inspecting the torched mattress. He touches the metal springs. "The culprit was probably a mattress fire."

According to 2017 data from the National Fire Protection Association, by far the most frequent cause of home fires is cooking (49 percent), followed by heating (14 percent), electrical and lighting (10 percent), intentional (8 percent), smoking materials (5 percent), and then less common problems like equipment malfunctions. Or, if you ask Richter, the number one cause of fires is "human fucking stupidity."

Richter points to the remains of the ceiling. "This is modern construction," he says, waving at the two-by-fours in the roof structure. He explains that they're not assembled with nails and heavy fasteners, as in the old days, but instead they use little gusset plates, which are cheaper and heat faster. The heat causes them to fall out of the wood. When they fall out of the wood, the roof collapses.

Richter carefully steps through the wreckage, inspecting the ceiling and the walls and the floor. "In traditional construction," he tells me, "that ceiling joist would have been at least a two-by-six." These things matter. Older homes used bigger pieces of wood. As everyone who has made a campfire knows, the bigger the log, the longer it burns. And the construction industry has found more profit in using cheaper, lighter materials.

These newer buildings are kindling. Old-time firefighters know this from personal experience and scientific data. An organization called the UL Firefighter Safety Research Institute, comprising both engineers and firefighters, has one of the coolest missions on the planet: they set things on fire. They burn buildings under controlled conditions to glean insights on how best to battle fires, and in one seminal experiment, they burned two nearly identical living rooms. They were the same size. They had the same amount of furniture. Yet one room was built from traditional construction (also called heritage construction, or legacy construction), the kind Richter is talking about, and filled with common household items (sofa, clothes, books) made from wood and cotton and wool, just like Grandma's house. The other room contained modern stuff: a microfiber-covered polyurethane foam-filled sectional sofa, a faux wooden coffee table, a thirty-seven-inch flat-screen TV, and plastic tubs. As one of the advisers to the UL research group, a field instructor and fire chief named Peter Van Dorpe, told me, "The couch you're sitting on today has perhaps ten times more fuel potential as the couch your grandma was sitting on."

In both rooms, the scientists lit a candle. They ignited the sofa. Then they waited.

For Grandma's room, it took twenty-nine minutes and thirty seconds until a flashover, that terrifying moment when the room superheats to 1,100 degrees and almost certainly kills anyone inside. Twenty-nine minutes is a long time in the world of firefighting.

The modern room? Three minutes and thirty seconds.

This evolution in home construction—of both the buildings and the contents of buildings—has changed the nature of firefighting. "The equipment is better, the helmets are better, the boots are better, and the trucks are better," Jenkerson told me, echoing other firefighters. "But then, on the other side of that, the fires are burning ten times hotter. You have less time."

Every modern building, when lit on fire, has the potential to explode like a bomb. That brings us to one of the most crucial in-the-field decisions for any battalion chief: whether to play offense or defense. From across the burned room Richter does a bit of role-playing and pretends I'm the fire's incident commander. "Do you send them [the firefighters] forward? Quick! *What do you do?*" I would face a gauntlet of split-second decisions. *There's black smoke.* Do I use a direct interior attack? *The ceiling's about to collapse.* Do I switch to defense? *The room suddenly superheats.* What now? As incident commander, you must cycle through a list of variables that includes the potential for saving lives, the volume of fire, the volume of smoke, the fuel load, the risk to the firefighters, the property value in play, the risk of structural collapse, the oxygen left in the tanks, the type of construction, the available manpower, the backup water supply, the backup attack lines, the placement of ladders, the available escape points, the experience of the firefighters, the odds of success, and the odds of a flashover.

The framework boils down to "Risk a lot to save a lot," meaning you attack the seat of the fire if lives can be saved and you think you can win, but if the odds are bleak and the home is empty, why take the chance? Then again, are you sure the building is empty? It's 2:00 a.m. and you can't see. And how, exactly, do you balance the scales with property value on one side and the lives of firefighters on the other? Fire is elemental. So, too, is the question that the incident commander must implicitly answer on every call: *Is this worth the lives of my firefighters?* The question dips into ethics and philosophy. Do you risk firefighters for a sleek high-rise building, but not a low-income home? These are the questions being debated throughout the fire service, as many departments now embrace a more defensive mind-set, and are less willing to let firefighters charge into the flames.

St. Louis is not one of them. "We're an aggressive fire department," Jenkerson told me in our very first conversation, and I would hear the same thing from dozens of St. Louis firefighters. *Aggressive, aggressive, aggressive.* They like to play offense. They like to attack. They do not discriminate between a wealthy house and a poor house. They don't think of them as houses; they think of them as homes. On 80 percent of Richter's calls, he directs an aggressive attack.

And that's what happened here. Because the firefighters attacked the seat of the fire, the flames were contained to one floor. Part of the home survived. And the neighbors survived. As we leave the building, Richter points to the adjacent homes, which are just inches apart. Thanks to the firefighters, the flames were unable to jump to the neighboring buildings. This fire lacked a cinematic "rescuing-a-baby" moment, but the firefighters possibly saved lives—we'll never know—and almost certainly prevented the destruction of two more houses—or rather two more homes.

As we leave, Richter looks back at the burned building, gives a nod. "That's what I call a good stop."

## Jack-of-All-Trades, Master of Tons

10:13 A.M.

Today's firefighters not only have to grapple with the challenges of new construction; they also must stay abreast of new technologies. This is why, at midmorning, Ramon's company heads to a training session. Every day they either do training like this or canvass their territory to inspect and familiarize themselves with buildings, which makes firefighters bristle at the notion that they're sitting around the firehouse, watching TV.

St. Louis has a new trolley system that, after years of delays, is finally up and running. When the trolley inevitably crashes? The fire department will be called. So Ramon and the other Truck 30 firefighters—Tyler, Willy, and Captain Kevin Duffy—head to the trolley headquarters to learn about things like the fuse boxes, emergency exits, and stopping speeds. They're joined by firefighters from a neighboring county.

"Where are the batteries located?" one asks, staring intently at the trolley.

"Where's the manual crank?" another asks.

"Is the battery 800 or 600 volts?"

I'm awed by how much stuff these guys need to know. They have to understand precisely how to de-energize a trolley, because if you first spray it with water, it might explode. (This is also the case with lithium batteries, so a fire in a Tesla, say, will only get more lethal with water.) On other days they'll brush up on the finer points of solar panels, elevators, freight trains, gas lines, and chemical warehouses. Every new technology brings new hazards. "If you look at the glorified heroes of the fire service from one hundred years ago, they would faint in awe from all the things we do today," says Tom Jenkins, the Arkansas fire chief.

Soon Ramon's radio crackles to life; it's a medical call. The guys race to the truck and Willy, the driver, flips on the sirens. The call is for a stroke, so Ramon slips on a pair of white latex gloves, his uniform for EMS runs. Ramon and Tyler will assess the potential stroke victim using the Cincinnati Pre-Hospital Stroke Scale (CPSS), asking the patient to smile so firefighters can see if one side of the face droops; a droop is a clue that one side of the brain is not working. Their range of expertise is astonishing. Earlier they studied the mechanics of trolley hydraulics, and now they're testing for neurological damage. I ask Ramon if this medical call is fairly routine.

"Nothing's routine," he says. That's a statement repeated many times: Nothing is routine. Things go sideways. On one recent stroke call, for example, Ramon helped a retired nun. The nun was mostly naked. She had lower gastrointestinal bleeding, so her bare legs and the floor were covered in liquid stool, which looked like "coffee grinds mixed with blood."

This is the grit that firefighters see every day. Most firefighters in the nation are now trained in EMS, and in St. Louis, you're required to obtain an EMS certification—120 hours of classes, plus clinical work—within your first year on the track. (On the track: firefighter for "in the field," or out in the streets doing work.) Firefighter after firefighter told me the same thing: If you're not interested in medical calls, don't become a firefighter.

Over the past few decades, fire departments have absorbed EMS into their portfolios. The roots of the emergency medical services date to the 1970s. As the highway system expanded, we drove more miles and crashed more cars. So we needed more first responders. Fire stations, which are distributed in a logical pattern on the map, serve as natural hubs for EMS. And then there's the money. EMS brings revenue to a fire department. "Fire chiefs seeking to preserve basic fire protection capacity in the wake of declining fire calls often fund the fire response end of the operation by providing EMS," writes Bruce Hensler in *Crucible of Fire: Nineteenth-Century Urban Fires and the Making of the Modern Fire Service*. "For cash-strapped local governments, any service with the potential to generate revenue is attractive, especially in a time of declining fires."

When you close your eyes and imagine a firefighter saving a life, you likely picture them carrying a child from the flames. That's what we see in the movies. And, yes, plenty of veteran firefighters, like Jenkerson and Richter, do have archetypical firefighter stories. Yet those are rare. In Fire Chief Tom Jenkins's entire career, for example, he has only seen a handful of people dragged from a burning building. All of them died. "But we'll save a dozen lives, at least, in the next twenty-four hours on medical runs," says Jenkins. "We save lives every dang day, but for some reason we [as a society] don't fancy it as sexy. We're the only health care professionals making house calls, and we do a damn good job of it."

## Changing the Culture

11:00 A.M.

In St. Louis, every fire alarm summons five trucks, one hook and ladder, one rescue squad, one ambulance, and two battalion chiefs. This means there are automatically between thirty and thirty-five firefighters on the scene. To minimize confusion, each company—a company is a truck or an engine, which has four firefighters—is automatically assigned a responsibility, based on the order in which they arrive on the scene. The captain of the company that gets there first, or "first in," needs to do a size-up—a quick 360-degree inspection of the building—and then heads in to attack the fire.

Just as every company has a responsibility, each of the company's four firefighters has an assigned role. Typically the lowest-ranking firefighter, like Ramon, is the "plug man"; his job is to connect the hose to a fire hydrant, or "make the plug," an expression dating back to a time when the water system was cobbled together from hollowed-out logs, and you pulled out a wooden plug to tap into the water.

The driver's job is to stay with the truck and operate the water supply, and in a pinch he helps the plug man. The leadoff man's job is to grab a hose and enter the building first, blasting the flames with water. The captain enters the building with a pickax. Like linebackers and cornerbacks who know their defensive assignments cold, every firefighter knows their duty. Other departments' standing operating guidelines (SOGs) will differ on the specifics, but the playbooks are similar.

Every time Ramon hops on the truck, he brings the SCBA. He explains that underneath the oxygen tank, in the back of the harness, is a bailout system that can unspool a rope that lets you rappel down a burning building. For this clever piece of kit, Ramon can thank fellow St. Louis firefighter and rescue squad leader Captain Mario Montero.

In an especially cold winter of 2003, when he was a captain of Engine House 29, Mario responded to a house fire in northern St. Louis. His truck was second in—that is, the second to arrive. Because of the department's SOGs, he knew exactly what he needed to do without being told.

It was cold that day—so cold that the first-in company, responsible for spraying water, had their hoses freeze. Since Mario's company was second in, his responsibility was search and rescue and helping with ventilation. Ventilation sounds simple but can be complex and deadly; cracking open windows and punching holes in the roof can lower the building's temperature, clear the deadly smoke and toxins, trim the risk of flashover, and improve visibility, but it can also feed the fire with more airflow. The timing can be tricky.

Mario entered with his pickax. He climbed the stairs to

the second floor. Not much smoke. It was the kind of fire he'd seen a hundred times before. He climbed to the third floor. It was pitch-black. Heavy smoke. Yet he didn't feel much heat on his ears—the ears are thin and can detect heat faster than the rest of your body—so he still wasn't too worried. In one bedroom there was a small window that needed ventilating. Mario smashed the window by ramming the head of his ax through it. Another firefighter on Mario's crew, Steve, was in the same room and smashed another window.

Then Mario felt the air change. Suddenly the room grew hot. Flames blasted into the room. With no warning, a red inferno erupted between Mario, who stood at the window, and the bedroom door—his only exit. Mario didn't have a hose. He was pinned at the window.

"*Mayday! Mayday! Mayday!*" Mario called out to the firefighters below, standing outside the building.

The fire approached.

Steve joined Mario at the window and also screamed for help. The flames reached both men. "I'm burning the fuck up!" Steve yelled. "I need to get the fuck out of here!"

There was no good way to escape. If they ran through the fire, they would die. The window was the only option, but on the third floor, at a height of thirty feet, a jump could cripple or kill. Life is not an action movie.

On the ground below, as soon as Mario called Mayday, a

quick-thinking firefighter tried to get a ladder in place. That firefighter happened to be Dennis Jenkerson, then a battalion chief. In the 2-degree winter air, a sheet of ice coated the ground. Jenkerson and another firefighter moved the ladder in place and held on like hell, knowing that the ladder, only twenty-four feet long, wouldn't quite reach the window and that the trapped firefighters would need to jump on it and pray.

There wasn't time to be graceful. Steve dove from the window, headfirst, and collided first into the ladder and then into Jenkerson, knocking him to the ground and tearing his rotator cuff. (Jenkerson went back to work the next day, just like his grandfather.)

Now Mario stood at the window. Behind him a ball of flame roared, silhouetting him in red. Mario had no choice; he had to bail. He climbed from the window and hung there, hands clinging to the windowsill. He hoped to drop onto the ladder and then climb down. His hands caught on fire. He had to let go.

It felt like he was falling to the ground in slow motion, and Mario watched the bricks of the wall pass by him, brick by brick. He knew that he would miss the ladder and drop the entire thirty feet. While falling he told himself, almost as a mantra, *It's not going to hurt, it's not going to hurt, it's not going to hurt . . .*

He landed. His first thought: *Oh. That fucking hurt.*

His second thought: *I'm paralyzed.*

Then he moved a foot. Moved a knee. Moved a leg. *Thank God.* He would walk again.

The fall did not kill him, but it did break his back. He was rushed to the hospital and stayed there for days, stuffed into a body brace, and then he faced months of physical therapy.

Mario worked hard on his recovery and he returned to the track with zero restrictions, but still, even today, his back is not whole. It never will be. "We can guarantee you're going to reinjure your back," the doctor told him. "We just don't know when it's going to happen." The pain is erratic. Mario will go months without feeling discomfort, and then for a few months he'll endure daily jolts of pain. Mario is adamant that the injury does not impact the way he does his job, but he knows he's at risk. "If I have to jump again—if something bad happens that second time—I'll be paralyzed," he says. "There's no more margin for error."

How dangerous is firefighting? Eighty-two firefighters died in 2018, each one a tragedy, but that number was also an "improvement" over the annual average of 127 in the 1980s. Perhaps the job is getting safer, but it's still deadly. Every death of a firefighter shakes the department. In 2002 two St. Louis firefighters, Captain Derek Martin and Captain Robert Morrison, lost their lives in a burning building, and their photos still hang in Firehouse 1, their old firehouse, which is Mario's current firehouse. They were family. They are still family. When Mario shows me their photos, this tough-as-steel firefighter isn't able to hide his emotion.

Yet, to directly address a spouse or parent's obvious question about firefighting—*"Are you going to die?"*—it can be useful, if a touch crass, to look at the cold numbers. How likely is it that a firefighter will die on the job? There are 1.1 million firefighters in the United States, including paid and volunteer departments. (The eighty-two deaths include thirty-three from paid departments, forty-four from volunteer departments, and five from wildland firefighters.) So if asked to calculate the chances, an emotionless robot might crunch the numbers and say, "Eighty-two deaths per every 1.1 million firefighters means that, on average, each year, a firefighter has a 0.01 percent chance of dying, or a 99.9 percent chance of living."

There are four problems with that math.

First, the robot is a dick. Second, those odds are only for one year. If you serve a full forty-year career, that 0.01 percent leaps to 0.3 percent—which sounds tiny, but it means that, over the course of forty years, one out of every three hundred firefighters will die. (The math is a bit oversimplified, but the principle holds.) Would you go on a cruise with three hundred people if you knew that one of you is certain to drown?

The third thing: those numbers overlook incidents like Mario's fall from the window. Mario is an exceptional firefighter. His nickname is "Super Mario," and he was featured in the photo essay book (photos by Paul Mobley, text by Joellen Kelly) called *American Firefighter*. Mario did nothing wrong. Yet sometimes shit goes sideways and you break your back. There are 80,000 injuries on the fire service each year, meaning roughly 7 percent of all firefighters get hurt on the job. Every time the bell goes off, there's a chance that your body will break or burn.

Ironically, Mario normally carried a tool that would have saved his back: it's the emergency bailout system, with a slim coil of rope that enables a firefighter to rappel down a window in scenarios precisely like this. (At the time, the bailout system was not a piece of gear issued by the department but an extra personal device that he usually brought with him, just in case.) On that winter day in 2003, Mario happened to leave the bailout system on the truck; he had never needed it before, so what were the odds he would need it in this particular emergency? "I was complacent," he tells me now. "I was complacent, and it bit me in the butt."

Jenkerson was at that fire. He saw the danger with his own eyes. And now he embraces a new philosophy, which is also the direction of the modern fire service: *One hundred deaths a year is too many. Eighty-two deaths is too many. One death is too many.*

*We can do better.* More departments now challenge the concept of "acceptable loss." When Jenkerson took over as fire chief, he carved out space in the budget to have the bailout system installed in every firefighter's SCBA so they will always have it in a fire. It's now part of their standard operating guidelines. When Ramon went through the academy, on the walls of the tower, he practiced using the bailout system to escape from windows. He hasn't had to use it yet, but you never do until your life—or your back—depends on it.

And now, finally, there's that fourth problem with the dick robot math: it excludes what might be the sneakiest and deadliest threat to firefighters—cancer.

To UNDERSTAND THE THREAT of cancer in the fire service, it helps to spend time in the lobby of the St. Louis Fire Department headquarters. The room is calm and quiet. There are no blaring sirens; there is no gunning of truck engines; there are no signs that lives are at stake. At the reception desk a nice lady sells candy and soda for a fundraiser that buys gifts for underprivileged children.

The lobby is also a museum that honors the department's rich history, which dates back to before the Civil War. Glass cabinets display antique helmets, newspaper clippings from the 1940s ("Fire Chief Morgan Dies a Hero, Saving the

Lives of His Men"), and miniatures of horse-drawn steam pumpers, which were still in use until the early twentieth century. A statue of Saint Florian, the patron saint of the fire service, stands vigil over the lobby. Florian, a Roman soldier who lived from circa AD 250 to 304, was allegedly the first to organize soldiers into firefighting units. (Fun fact: when Florian was revealed to be a Christian—then frowned upon—the authorities tied him to a stake and threatened to burn him over a pyre. As they were about to light the pyre, Florian shouted, "If you do, I will climb to heaven on the flames!" They listened to him, considered this, and then drowned him instead.)

In one of the lobby's paintings, you can see what a fire scene looked like in the 1800s: St. Louis residents kept wooden buckets in their homes, and if their buildings caught on fire, they tossed their buckets out their windows into the street, and the firefighters filled the buckets with water— using the same kind of wooden hand pumps employed by Benjamin Franklin's volunteers in the 1730s. (Apologies to your high school history teacher, but Benjamin Franklin did not organize America's first fire service. The first volunteer fire department in North America dates back to 1658, when Peter Stuyvesant organized the eighty-man New Amsterdam fire company, the distant ancestor of the FDNY.)

But back to the STLFD headquarters lobby. The legendary firemen depicted in these scenes, from the 1800s through the 1980s, all had some things in common. They were all brave, they all saved lives, and they were all tough sons of bitches. And they did it all without modern SCBAs and flame-resistant bunker gear. Yet there's something else: they were all dirty.

"Firefighting is a tough, dirty, nasty job," Jenkerson tells me in his office. In the era of his father and his grandfather, "working dirty" was a badge of honor. Charging into the fire without a mask meant you were a real man. If you're coughing? If you can't breathe? *Suck it up.*

A generation ago, firefighters waged their battles in homes made of wood and brick. "It was all natural-made stuff," says Jenkerson. This is the same point Richter made before, and it's so elemental to modern firefighting that it's worth repeating. "Nowadays, you go into a house, and it's all man-made products. The carpeting. The furniture. Everything is plastic," says Jenkerson. Even a simple fire in a trash can means the burning of plastic yogurt cups, plastic bag liners, plastic take-out containers. All of this emits carcinogens. "Look at automobiles: they're all plastic," the fire chief points out. "We used to have steel cars. Not anymore. Everything is a carcinogen."

The toxins, carcinogens, and smoke are absorbed through the skin as well as the respiratory system. Jenkerson knows this from personal experience. One night decades ago, when he was still a young firefighter, his unit caught a fire with heavy smoke. The next morning, when off duty, he and the captain played racquetball. Afterward they hit the sauna. They were joined by another guy, a non-firefighter. The guy sniffed and looked around the sauna and said, "Something's burning." The smell was so thick that he left, worried about a fire. Jenkerson and his captain chuckled a bit. There was no fire; the smell came from the smoke oozing from their skin.

Jenkerson no longer chuckles. He has seen the grim statistics, and he knows that firefighters are more likely to die of cancer than non-firefighters. Three times more likely, according to an alarming 2018 study from the University of Central Lancashire, in Preston, UK. In the past three years alone, Jenkerson's department has lost ten firefighters—all under the age of fifty—to cancer, which dwarfs the number of firefighters who have died in the line of duty (two) since he took over in 2007. "And it's all because of the by-products of the smoke," he says.

So Jenkerson launched a safety campaign, called Boots Off, meant to hammer home the fact that firefighters are more likely to die with their boots off—in a hospital bed, with cancer—than they are in a flaming building. Over the course of three days (in order to hit the A, B, and C shifts)

Jenkerson called every one of his 587 firefighters into a classroom. He wanted to "scare the living hell out of these guys."

The message: You will no longer be considered a "real man" for barreling into a smoking building without wearing a mask. You will keep clean. The department now issues each firefighter two sets of turnout gear so that, after a fire, one can be washed immediately to rinse away the toxins. One of Jenkerson's to-dos this afternoon, in fact, is to review an $880,000 federal grant to help pay for the extra turnout gear. Every fire truck is now equipped with baby wipes. (Peter Van Dorpe, the UL research board adviser, notes that departments are doing this around the country, "except they don't call them baby wipes; they call them 'rescue wipes.'")

Jenkerson says that, prior to the Boots Off campaign, firefighters would emerge from a smoking building, head straight to the Red Cross or Salvation Army canteen, and wolf down some cookies; as a result, they were "washing the carcinogens down their gut." Now firefighters are forced to wash and clean up before they eat or drink—or, as Jenkerson says in his Missouri accent, "warsh and clean up." He even gave an edict to the Red Cross and Salvation Army: Don't give food or drink to these firefighters if they haven't cleaned up first. "It's simple stuff."

Every year the firefighters are required to get a physical. Jenkerson prepared a letter requiring additional cancer screenings that every firefighter must bring to their doctor. Thanks to these letters, multiple firefighters caught early-stage colon cancer.

These initiatives reflect nationwide trends in the fire service, and are in the same spirit as the work of the National Fallen Firefighters Foundation, which, in 2004, developed sixteen safety initiatives to help reach the ultimate goal of zero firefighter deaths. The initiatives include risk management, psychological support, near-miss investigations, and cultural change.

That final initiative is the fire chief's core message: "We're trying to change the culture so that a dirty firefighter is not a good firefighter." But he knows it's a tough sell. "There's an old saying," he tells me. " 'Firefighters hate the status quo, but they also hate change.' "

## II

——

## Afternoon

## From Lunch to the Flophouse

Noon

Lunchtime. Here's how meals work in most station houses in St. Louis: firefighters do their own thing for breakfast (Ramon skips the meal but munches on a bag of Cheetos), and then they do a combination daily grocery run for both lunch and dinner. Lunch is fend-for-yourself; dinner is communal.

Ramon's Truck 30 usually makes two stops for groceries: a wholesale joint where they buy their chicken or beef in bulk, and then the amazingly named Schnucks, a St. Louis supermarket franchise, for everything else. This keeps the cost of dinner to under $6 per person.

Who cooks the meals? Like so much in the fire service, this varies by firehouse. Sometimes they rotate. Sometimes one firefighter who enjoys cooking does it every time. Sometimes it's the new prick. On top of the nightly dinner costs, each month the firefighters chip in $20 for some basics around the firehouse: coffee, salad dressing, cooking oil, dishrags, soap. They also pay for their own cable and Wi-Fi, which is a minor grievance, and it's a retort to those who complain about firefighters "wasting taxpayer dollars." How many jobs do you know where the employees buy office light bulbs?

On this errand to buy groceries, as in all errands, the firefighters travel together. This sounds inefficient, even a bit ridiculous—four firefighters to buy a sack of potatoes?— but the squad must stay together, always, no matter how trivial the outing. Calls happen anytime. If you send the new prick to buy a chicken and then catch a call, suddenly you've lost your plug man.

Inside Schnucks, Ramon listens to the department radio as he checks the price of chicken wings. Ramon is not a man who craves variety. Every day he eats chicken wings for lunch, grilling a triple-size portion so he can share with the house. All firefighters listen to the radio at all times, from the fire chief to the new prick. The radio has a transcendent power to change your day on a dime. It's almost a game. Can we finish shopping before we catch a call? We make it to the front of the store, then to the cash register. We're almost home free . . . and then Ramon's radio hisses to life: "*Truck 30, respond.*"

Ramon leaves the chicken with the cashier. "We'll be back!" We jog out of the store and hop in the truck.

The call is another EMS run. We'll go on several more EMS calls throughout the day. They begin to blur together. For every medical call, Willy flips on the sirens and Tyler and Ramon, sitting in the back of the truck, slip on the white latex gloves. On one call, the truck pulls up to a dialysis center, and the firefighters help an eighty-four-year-old African American woman in a wheelchair who had earlier fainted. Ramon checks her blood pressure: 140 over 70.

"Ma'am, are you feeling okay?" Ramon asks.

The woman, confused and exhausted, doesn't answer.

"Ma'am, how many years young are you?" Tyler asks with a respectful smile.

She still doesn't answer. Ramon, Tyler, and Captain Duffy gently ask her some questions to baseline her mental condition: "Ma'am, what year is it?" A blank stare. "Do you know who the president is?" Another blank stare. "What's your address, ma'am?" Something clicks: she gives her address right away.

The lady looks like she might pass out, but it's not clear if they're dealing with dementia or low blood sugar or something more troubling. An ambulance pulls up; the medics will take it from here. This is often the job of a firefighter at an EMS scene: basic first aid until the medics arrive, as the fire department usually arrives first. Ramon and Tyler lift the nice lady from the wheelchair to a stretcher, and the medics whisk her away to the hospital. What happened to her after that? They don't know and never will.

In another call, while en route, Tyler glances at the Active911 app and checks the address. "A frequent flyer," he says, and then translates for me: "Frequent flyer. We come here a lot. It's a flophouse."

At the apartment building they head upstairs and find a woman with no pants on, trying to stick her arm through the neck of her shirt. She just completed rehab and now she overdosed on heroin.

The squad sees a lot of heroin overdoses. Jenkerson estimates that the fire department treats ten overdoses a day, and in almost every one of these calls the response by the department saves a life. They see so many overdoses that Ramon's supervisor, Captain Kevin Duffy, says he knows the patterns so well, he can tell when a new heroin shipment has arrived. They find victims in the park, in the street, in abandoned buildings.

The firefighters treat overdoses with Narcan, a brand name for naloxone, which is sprayed into the nose by means of a plastic device the size of an asthma inhaler. Naloxone blocks opioid receptors and instantly revives the patient. Sometimes the patient is angry that their high has been cut short. Sometimes the firefighter treats the same frequent flyer multiple times in a day: overdose, revival, overdose, revival. "It's self-inflicted," one firefighter told me, exasperated. He says he will always do his job, and he will always be professional, but the overdose calls are a special kind of frustration. He says, partly in jest, that every time they respond to an OD call, they should use a Magic Marker to put a big X on the frequent flyer's forehead, and when they get three X's . . . He leaves the rest unsaid. "Still, it's our job," he adds. "We're saving those people's lives."

## Hands On

12:30 P.M.

The job of a firefighter is one of the most physically grueling professions on the planet, demanding a mix of brute
strength, endurance, dexterity, and more brute strength. To
get a better sense of the physical burden, I asked the STLFD
to put me through some basic drills.

So, just after lunch, Richter brings me to yet another
vacant home with broken windows, a shattered door, and
walls that are charred and cracked. I'm wearing a firefighter's
turnout gear. It took me five minutes to squeeze my body into
the thick rubber boots, suspenders, and coat. With a bit of
awe, I fasten that hard bucket of a helmet onto my head, and
tighten the chin strap until the helmet stops wiggling. It's
hard to move my head and hard to move my body. In the July
heat I'm sweating within seconds.

Richter hands me a pike pole, a long wooden shaft that's
topped with a spear and a hook.

First introduced in the 1600s, the pike pole was once used
to grab hunks of buildings and place them in the path of a fire,
in the hopes of preventing its spread. This is the hook that
spawned the term "hook and ladder." It remains the go-to
tool for the critical task of overhaul: while some firefighters
blast the flames with water, others use pike poles to rip out

Sheetrock (to search for flames lurking in the walls), break windows (to ventilate), and snatch objects from the flames.

Richter points to a slab of plywood that covers a broken window on the home's front wall. "Rip out that plywood," Richter tells me, his voice stern and gruff.

"Chief?"

"Rip it out."

I stab the corner of the plywood. I can't get it to stick.

Richter paces a bit, cigarette in mouth. He watches me in silence, stern, poker-faced.

I stab the plywood a few more times and finally get some leverage, dislodging a chunk, heaving with all of my body. I pause for breath and then another tiny chunk of wood comes off. Soon I'm gassed. Finally I peel off the entire board, and a few of Richter's firefighters, who have gathered around to watch, give me some good-natured, if slightly sarcastic, claps. A real firefighter would pop this board in seconds.

We enter the broken home. Richter points upward. "Overhaul the ceiling."

I stab the plaster of the ceiling. Debris hits me in the face. I keep stabbing. More debris. Soon it's difficult to see from all the dust.

"Keep going," Richter says, his voice flat, commanding. My shoulders beg for mercy. Jenkerson tells me that a firefighter's shoulders take the biggest pounding. It requires real effort to strike the ceiling repeatedly, and I've only done a few feet. In a typical fire you'd overhaul multiple rooms and you'd do it with poor visibility, breathing through your mask, listening to your radio for the captain's instructions, and making sure you don't fall through the floor. And you'd do it knowing that at any moment you could die.

RICHTER HAS ME SWING an ax, yank Sheetrock, and break windows—which, to be perfectly honest, is kind of the best thing ever. But the drills leave me humbled and exhausted. I have the same reaction when Captain Mario Montero gives me a taste of what it's like to crawl through a fire.

We're on his home turf, Engine House 1. In addition to the standard bunker gear, I'm also wearing a SCBA. I don the hood, strap on the mask, and breathe like Darth Vader. It's hard to see through the plastic.

"You ready to go into the fire?" Mario asks.

No. I nod yes.

"This is what it will look like."

He takes a bag and puts it over my head. Darkness.

"Now, quick, get on your knees!" Mario swings opens the door. I get as low to the ground as possible, "sucking the floor" to stay under the extreme heat.

"Move forward!" Mario says. "Follow me." I scramble to

keep up with him, crawling while staying low—not easy with fifty pounds of gear.

"Are there survivors?" Mario asks. "You gotta check!"

I sweep the ground with one hand, using my arm like a windshield wiper, which is how you do search and rescue when it's too dark to see. I flail about, trying to keep my butt low. "Okay, now I want you to go back the way you came," Mario says.

Shit. "I'm not sure where that is," I admit.

"Well, you better find it."

In front of me: darkness. Behind me: darkness. I begin to panic. This little drill of Mario's is the gentlest of exercises, as we are, in fact, safely in the sleeping quarters of Engine House 1, with no smoke, no heat, no flames, no risk of injury, no lives at stake . . . and still it kicked my ass.

Now I'm the Plug Man. This is Ramon's job at a fire. I'm sitting inside the pumper, once again in turnout gear, and the truck drives a few blocks, then lurches to a stop.

"Go, go, go!" Mario yells. "Move it, plug man!"

I grab a Hydra-Shield—a sort of supersized wrench for the fire hydrant—and climb down from the truck and hustle to the back, where I grab the four-inch-diameter hose and toss it over my shoulder.

"Run! Run!"

I take off with the hose at a dead sprint. Within seconds I slow as the hose gets heavier—so much heavier—as it unspools from the truck. Every 100-foot section of the hose weighs eighty-five pounds. Add to that friction from the concrete.

"Run!" Mario yells, but all I can manage is a slow jog. My legs protest. My shoulders give. I've hauled only one and a half sections, or 150 feet, and it feels like I'm trying to drag the truck itself across the concrete. Then I can move no more. The other firefighters jump in to help—firefighters are wired to help—and finally, with their added muscle, I pull the hose to the hydrant. Out of breath, my hands shaking, I use the Hydra-Shield to break the seal. The water gushes from the hydrant. Thank God. I fasten the hose and make the plug. I'm spent.

"At a real fire," Mario says, "your work would just begin. Now you'd go inside the house."

I'm in decent physical shape. I regularly run four miles, play tennis, lift weights. I served in the U.S. Marine Corps Forces Reserve and I went to boot camp. But these firefighting maneuvers are some of the most physically demanding things I've ever done in my life.

———

IN THE ABANDONED BUILDING, Richter has me do a "mule kick," where you stand in front of a closed and locked door, lift your knee, and then strike out behind you. It takes me a few tries.

An example of when the mule kick can come in handy: years ago, Richter caught the kind of fire where you can't see the flames from the outside—only puffs of dark smoke. These are tricky. Veteran firefighters know that "Hollywood fires," with their bright and cinematic flames, can be less threatening than a dark and smoking building. As one firefighter put it, with heavy smoke "you can't see shit" and it's harder to find the seat of the fire.

When Richter arrived at the smoking building, the other firefighters still hadn't entered. A crowd of neighbors hovered near the front door. The leadoff man tried to mule-kick the door. It wouldn't budge. He tried again. It still wouldn't budge. Richter heard that a woman might be trapped inside.

Richter told the crowd to move aside. They didn't seem to understand, as many were Bosnian—St. Louis has one of the largest Bosnian populations outside of Europe—and struggled with English. He glared at them. "Get the fuck out of here!" They still didn't get it. "Get the fuck out!" he yelled. "As soon as I open the doorway, flames are going to come out!" That somehow clicked and they moved away from the door.

Richter pushed the leadoff man out of the way and mule-kicked the door himself. Instantly it shattered. He crouched and entered the building. Smoke filled the room. An upholstered sofa was in flames, unleashing the kind of toxic black smoke that can wreak havoc on your lungs. Richter wasn't wearing a mask but he didn't care. He crawled as low as he could. All he could see was darkness and flames and then, near the floor, a slice of clear air. (Imagine trying to watch a movie, but the only thing you can see is the bottom edge of the screen, and then you need to extrapolate the rest of the action.) Those few inches of visibility were enough: he spotted a foot. He belly crawled and found the woman.

"Was she conscious?" I ask.

"Fuck no," says the chief. He dragged her to the main room, still keeping low, and then charged to the front door, where a crowd of firefighters blocked his way. "Get the fuck out of the way! Man with a baby!" ("Man with a baby" is code for saving someone from the fire.)

He carried the woman outside. It was cold. There was snow on the ground. The chief dropped her into the snow and gave her CPR.

She gasped for air. She would live. Soon the paramedics came to relieve him, but Richter's job wasn't done. He grabbed a pike pole and headed back into the smoking building, where he smashed the walls and helped to ventilate the smoke.

Four months later the department gave Richter a Distinguished Service Cross. "I didn't think much of it," Richter says. "You must be hard up for giving out medals if you're giving one to me."

Richter is uncomfortable telling these kinds of stories. To him it feels like bragging, and the chief is not a bragger. Before I coaxed it out of him, this is how he told me the story: "One time we went to a fire. I kicked in the door. I crawled around, found a lady, and dragged her to the front yard. She lived."

That was the fifth or "maybe sixth" person Richter saved from a fire. There were more. He's lost count.

## The Nerve Center

1:30 P.M.

Today is a relatively slow day. By this time in a typical day, Richter will have received seven emergency calls, Ramon two or three, and Jenkerson's St. Louis Fire Department more than eighty. These calls are routed to the Fire Dispatch, a small office in the Fire Department headquarters. The dispatch room is packed with four desks and twenty-odd computer monitors. It looks a bit like NASA Mission Control.

Moments after I pop my head in the room, a dispatcher named Rodney fields a call. A sixteen-year-old boy has been shot, and Rodney is now talking to the boy's sister, who witnessed the shooting. Rodney doesn't know if the shooter is still on the scene.

"Where's your mom? . . . Okay. Try and be calm . . . Wait a minute, hold up. Don't run down there. You don't know if the shooter is still down there . . . Do you see your mother? . . . Slow down . . . Don't run in the middle of the street where your brother got shot! If they're still down there shooting, we don't want you to get hit . . . Wait a minute. Wait a minute. Try to calm down . . . He got shot in the leg? . . . Where's your mom? You go back to the house! . . . Hey, hey, hey! Little girl! Listen, listen, listen. Stop screaming. Where's your mom? . . . Tell your mother you're talking to 911. Put her on the phone . . ."

Rodney's voice is urgent yet empathetic. Meanwhile, the other two dispatchers calmly work at their own desks, focused on their computers, nonplussed by what might be the most harrowing phone call I've ever heard. One woman eats from a fruit cup.

Rodney continues the call.

"Little girl, don't hang up! . . . Is your brother moving? . . . He is? Okay. Don't hang up. Calm down . . ."

A pause. I'm guessing the mother is now on the phone.

"Ma'am, this is the fire department. We're on the way. How many times has he been shot? . . . We're on the way . . . Where was he shot at? Upper leg or lower leg? . . . Above the knee or below the knee? . . ."

While Rodney is on the phone, he codes in the emergency to the computer, which automatically triggers an ambulance or fire truck to be dispatched.

The three-person team fields two hundred calls a day, including one recent call where the dispatcher talked someone through delivering a baby. "It gets a little crazy here," she told me, laughing a bit.

These dispatchers make the split-second decisions on which company is summoned, whether it's a first-alarm or second-alarm fire, and so on. This is the brain that zaps neurons to the rest of the fire department's body. Much of it is computerized. Scrolling through a list of variables, the system's algorithm suggests the optimal resource to be deployed—which company is closest? What if they're out on another call? Is traffic blocking the route?—but the dispatchers use common sense to occasionally override the system.

Today, a firefighter named Licole McKinney is training to be a dispatcher. This is a bit of cross-functional training the department encourages, which both (a) gives the chiefs versatility in balancing work schedules (if they're short-handed at Dispatch, they can now plug in Licole), and (b) gives Licole some extra overtime on her off days.

Licole only recently began the training—it will take several months—but she already has plenty of friends at Dispatch. "Ask her about the car fire," Rodney tells me. "Ask her!"

———

A FEW YEARS BACK, Licole's Saturday began quietly enough: she was thinking about waffles. On weekends the firefighters at Engine House 33 do a family-style breakfast. While driving to work, Licole hoped that one of her squad mates, Vincent, would remember to bring the waffle maker.

Then she saw the car. It was across the street and it was on fire. Immediately she turned the wheel and sped to the scene.

Two other off-duty firefighters had also spotted the flames and rushed to help. Through the flames, Licole saw that an unconscious man was trapped in the front seat. She knew that she didn't have any gear—no mask, no turnout gear, no helmet, no pike pole, no hose, and no water—but the car was on fire and a man was trapped inside. A crowd of onlookers had gathered, and one woman kept screaming, "It's going to blow! It's going to blow!"

Licole knew her fires. She knew she had a little more time. As a few citizens also moved in to help, Licole reached through the door into the car, grabbed the unconscious guy's shirt—burning her hands in the process—and lugged him out of the vehicle. She felt for a pulse. *Still alive*. She began chest compressions. She gave him CPR.

The entire front of the car now filled with flames . . . and then Licole saw another passenger. A woman was trapped, her foot somehow pinned between the car and the ground. The flames approached her leg. Her leg caught on fire. In an incredible stroke of luck, Vincent, Licole's squad mate, who had driven back home to fetch the waffle maker, had spotted the fire and stopped to help. So while Licole continued CPR on the unconscious guy, Vincent grabbed the woman's arms to pull her out. The woman's flesh, melting from the flames, peeled off her arms. Vincent managed to pull the woman out, but now her hair caught on fire. Licole leapt up to help, and started smacking the flames with her bare hands. (At this point Licole was joined by yet another firefighter from their squad, Frank, who also stopped to help.) Vincent took off his fleece sweatshirt and used it as a sort of blanket, smothering her in a bear hug.

Seconds after they grabbed the woman from the car, it became fully engulfed in flames. *No time to think about that.* Immediately Licole switched to medical mode. She started spiking the IV kits and treated the woman for trauma. (Licole had worked an ambulance for years.). The woman's foot was unrecognizable. As Licole remembers, it looked as if it had "been through a garbage disposal."

The woman would live. And the man would live. Licole and the other firefighters would be given Medals of Honor

and a proclamation from the city. *Firehouse* magazine cited them for bravery, and gave each firefighter $500. (Licole spent it on her daughter.) Yet, when she tells me the story, the main thing Licole stresses is that "I didn't do this alone. We work as a team." Virtually every firefighter said the same thing when sharing a story of how they saved a life: "We're a team." "This is just our job." "We're here to serve." "Teamwork, teamwork, teamwork." With other professions, this might sound like lip service. With firefighters, this is a cornerstone principle.

## Fire Prevention

2:30 P.M.

Back in Ramon's firehouse, a random guy strolls in and asks, "Hey, can I get a smoke alarm installed?"

"No problem," the captain tells him, and they schedule an installation without delay. No waiting in lines. No getting put on hold. Imagine getting that kind of customer service at, say, the cable company.

The entire interaction takes two minutes, but the seeds of the exchange began, in a sense, in the nineteenth century. In 1849, on a cargo steamer along the waterfront of St. Louis, someone dropped a lit cigarette. A fire started. The flames leapt to the next boat, then the next and then the next, feasting on the cargo of cotton, lumber, and hemp. A total of twenty-two steamers burned. The flames jumped to the docks and to the wooden houses near the water, then to the center of downtown. The volunteer fire department—at the time comprising nine hand-pumped, horse-drawn engines—did the best they could, but the city was made of wood, and much of the city burned to a crisp.

For centuries, fires like these regularly claimed lives. This spurred a growth in the fire service. "As U.S. cities rapidly expanded in the wake of industrialization in the 1800s, they burned with regularity, requiring a massive response in firefighting capacity," Bruce Hensler explains in *Crucible of Fire*. ". . . Cities had to be safe from fires to protect the financial investments of the private sector. The effort to preserve economic wealth resulted in the organized fire service we know today."

Yet the world still burned. In 1903, flames in the supposedly fireproof Iroquois Theater in Chicago killed 602. In 1911, the infamous fire in New York's Triangle Shirtwaist Factory killed 146 employees, mostly young women who jumped from tenth-story windows and fell to their deaths. In 1944, a fire at the Ringling Bros. and Barnum & Bailey Circus in Hartford, Connecticut, killed 168 and possibly more. Many of them were children.

We, as a society, are getting better at preventing these tragedies. As our population grows, the number of fires plummets. The recent surge of wildfires, of course, is the devastating outlier to this trend. The job of the U.S. Forest Service's wildland firefighters—around 10,000 in total, or roughly 1 percent of all firefighters—is a different enough beast to fall outside of this book's scope. In 1977, 3.3 million fires burned; forty years later that plunged to 1.3 million. We can thank a focus on fire prevention that includes building codes, sprinkler systems, and smoke alarms.

"Fire prevention is the most important thing we do," Jenkerson told me, adding that, in 1984, St. Louis was one of the first departments to proactively install smoke alarms, that each year they install 7,000 smoke alarms, and that they do it for free. In one study, smoke alarms slashed the risk of death by fire by more than 50 percent.

This is why Ramon isn't surprised when a random guy walks in and asks for a smoke alarm. And they're not at all surprised by our next call: another commercial fire alarm. They respond to many fire alarms, and each time they need to don the bunker gear, inspect the building, and take the threat of fire seriously.

It's usually a false alarm, but there are also calls like the one Ramon caught last week when he responded to an alarm in the upscale Central West End neighborhood. He entered the apartment to investigate. It was a nice place but cluttered with beer cans, trash, and dirty dishes. It smelled of urine. Ramon thought the place was empty, but then, across the room, he saw a guy on the couch, just sitting there, his head slumped over, with long black hair covering his face. He looked like Jesus.

Ramon worried that the guy needed help. He grabbed his radio. "Captain, we need to get a medical unit!"

The captain raced in. He inspected the man on the couch. Then he glared at the new prick. "Ramon, are you fucking stupid?"

"Sir?"

"You don't know how to tell a dead body?"

The guy had been dead for two weeks. Ramon moved closer and could now see that the feet were so swollen, so fat, that they were about to burst open; the body's fluids had drained through the legs and pooled into his ankles.

Every firefighter has stories like this—stories that rarely get told on the airbrushed, feel-good segments on the local news. Stories of body after body after body.

## Payday

3:30 P.M.

When he's not on a call, Richter likes to roam the district and do size-ups of buildings (to learn of any hazardous materials, say) and check up on his crew. A battalion chief's most important job, Richter tells me, is to know his people and his district.

Twice a month, on payday, he carries a stack of envelopes, like a mailman, and hand-delivers them to his stations. These are the firefighters' pay stubs. "They get direct deposit," Richter grumbles. "It's the stupidest thing ever."

Maybe that's the case, but the firefighters still tear open the envelopes, excited, eager to see the amounts. Each month the checks can change. And they're usually higher than their baseline salaries because of one magical word: "overtime." One firefighter opens the envelope and fist pumps. "Ninety-six hours!"

So, what's the pay like as a firefighter?

"You're not going to get rich," one firefighter told me, "but it can be a good living." I heard that line over and over, from chiefs to captains to new pricks, from firefighters in St. Louis and Chicago and New York. I heard it so much that it feels like an official fire service talking point: "Well, you're not going to get rich . . ."

In St. Louis, in every kitchen of the firehouse, a pay schedule is tacked onto the bulletin board. This is refreshingly transparent. Compare that to almost every other job in the United States, where you don't know if you're making more or less than the guy sitting next to you. The St. Louis pay grid (dated June 24, 2018) shows that a firefighter with no experience makes $47,815, and every year brings a small bump until year 30, capping at $67,887. That's if you never get promoted. Captains make between $73,000 and $82,000, battalion chiefs between $92,000 and $95,000, and the fire commissioner (Jenkerson) between $114,000 and $121,000. (Jenkerson's salary is telling: the person who is effectively the CEO—at the absolute peak of the pyramid—tops out in the low six figures. How many CEOs of $62 million companies pay themselves $121,000?)

One veteran battalion chief described the department's salaries as "middle-of-the-road" compared to the rest of the nation, and the numbers bear this out. The average firefighter's salary is $50,272, according to CareerExplorer.com, with New York paying the highest ($81,240) and Louisiana the skimpiest ($28,200). Veteran firefighters all tell me the same thing: Don't do this for the money. That said, in addition to the pension (which starts to kick in at year 20), there are a few factors that sweeten the pot:

1. **Stability.** No job is guaranteed, but firefighting is about as close as you can get to recession-proof. Even during the Great Recession of 2009, with the budget groaning, the St. Louis Fire Department enacted a hiring freeze—but not layoffs—which gradually shrank the department through attrition. Since then, it has inched back up to its pre-recession level of around six hundred. Adjusted for the U.S. population in general, over the last thirty years, the total number of firefighters has held steady.

2. **Overtime.** Jenkerson still has that shortage of paramedics ("paramedics, not combat medics"), and now the whole city knows it. Yet, even if he can hire more, St. Louis will always need firefighters to volunteer for OT, and most are delighted to oblige.

3. **Almost every firefighter has a second stream of income.** In St. Louis, every nine-day cycle looks like this: twenty-four hours on, twenty-four hours off, twenty-four hours on, twenty-four hours off, twenty-four hours on, and then four days off. Weekends lose relevance. Off time is not driven by Saturdays and Sundays, but by when your four-day break happens to fall, and that's always changing because nine-day cycles do not map cleanly into thirty- or thirty-one-day months. This can be tough on families and friends, and it's one reason firefighters tend to hang with other firefighters: their goofy schedules sync. There's no national standard for these cycles. In New York, for example, they run fourteen-hour shifts; in New Jersey it's twenty-four on and seventy-two off. The upshot is that these four consecutive off days are intended as an opportunity for firefighters to replenish their tanks. But many, if not all, use the four-day block as a time for their side gigs or to rack up some OT.

The side jobs run the gamut, from safety instructors to substitute teachers to actors to DJs. Ramon cuts grass on the side. Richter works construction and teaches classes on rope rescue. A firefighter's salary, buttressed with a second partial income, can provide a comfortable life.

But the larger point? Most firefighters don't do it for the money. "Find me another job in America where people in such large numbers are willing to do the job for nothing," says FDNY fire captain Jason Brezler. "There isn't one." He's referring to the 700,000 volunteer firefighters who do the job for free, on the side, while they work a nine-to-five job and live a normal life.

## The Challenge of Inclusion
4:30 P.M.

Licole finishes her stint at dispatch, then heads to her firehouse, Engine House 33, on the north side of St. Louis, just a few miles from the town of Ferguson. The neighborhood is high in shootings, heroin overdoses, and prostitution.

This doesn't seem to faze Licole. "I just treat everyone the same. When I treat everybody as if they're my family member, it's a lot easier for me. If you're elderly, I treat you like my grandfather," she says. She extends that same courtesy to the homeless and the call girls who loiter by the station. At 6:50 one morning, for example, a guy came to the firehouse requesting help: he had locked his keys in his car, just a block away. Could they open it for him?

"Sure," Licole told the guy. "No problem." Firefighters do

this kind of thing all the time. She grabbed some wedges and the BigEasy, a long, slender tool that's used to jimmy open the door. Then, at the car, she encountered a young woman yelling at the guy, saying he owed her twenty bucks.

"I don't owe you shit," the guy told her.

"I sucked your dick," said the woman. "You owe me twenty bucks."

On the ground by the car, Licole saw a purse, condoms, a crack pipe, lip gloss, and panties. Now it became clear: she figured the guy must have angrily thrown the prostitute's things on the ground and locked himself out of the car.

"Sir, do you owe this woman twenty bucks?"

"I don't owe this bitch shit."

"Sir, look. I'm not saying I condone what she does," Licole told him, "but I work hard for my money, too. And if you owe her twenty bucks, then you need to give her the money."

The man said that he had only a hundred-dollar bill. Licole pointed to a liquor store and told him that he could break the hundred and pay the lady.

"I'm not paying her shit."

So Licole gave an ultimatum: Either pay the lady the $20 or keep his $20 . . . and pay another $60 for a locksmith, because Licole wouldn't open the door. (She conferred with her captain and got his backing.)

"Thank you, Ms. Fire Lady!" the prostitute said.

Licole looks at me now, laughs a bit. "You don't *do* people like that. You pay the lady."

From that point on, the local prostitutes knew her as Auntie Licole.

Most of the stories involving sex workers aren't cute. Almost in the next breath, Licole tells me that the fire station made friends with a prostitute named Tiara. "She was a regular, and we loved her." She pauses, then adds, "A guy raped Tiara and killed her."

It's not lost on Licole that she is one of only fifteen female firefighters in the department. I can sense that she'd rather speak about actual firefighting, or EMS calls, or even Tiara than about gender issues, but she gamely agrees to share what it's like to be a female firefighter, the good and the bad.

Licole wants to stress that she loves the job. She loves her crew. She loves her people. "This is a very rewarding job," she says. "And I love that we're serving the community." Yet it's also undeniable that, especially early in her twenty-year career, she has had to conquer barriers that don't exist for male firefighters.

This is true across the nation. One 2008 study, *A National Report Card on Women in Firefighting*, conducted for the International Association of Women in Fire & Emergency Services, found that 84.7 percent of women reported being treated differently because of their gender; 50.8 percent reported high levels of shunning or isolation; 42.9 percent reported verbal harassment; and 30.2 percent reported sexual advances. More recently, in 2019, a survey of 2,022 female firefighters suggested that little has improved. The researchers found that "women reported experiencing verbal harassment (37.5 percent), written harassment (12.9 percent), hazing (16.9 percent), sexual advances (37.4 percent), and assaults (5.1 percent)." Nationwide, the fire service has had a disturbing record of sexual harassment, and it's likely that the actual numbers are higher than what has been reported.

Twenty years ago, while Licole was working at EMS, she had men try to kiss her, inappropriately hug her, grope her, and expose themselves to her. When she was first given a tour of one engine house, in the locker room, she was asked, "Want to give me a BJ?"

Licole reported this to a female captain and asked her, "What is it I need to do to get these men to leave me alone?" The female captain told her that because she (the captain) now knew of the incident, she was bound by law to report it. So the captain reported it. "But now I'm the problem child," says Licole. Even talking to me, for this book, is something of a risk for Licole, as she might be seen as the problem child. To be clear, she did not seek this conversation.

There were also what Licole calls "the little things. Subtle things." Years ago on a call, a firefighter asked her to bring him the K-12 rotary saw. She gave it to him. He tried to start the saw. It didn't start. There happened to be a crowd of police and firefighters on the scene, and the other firefighter was embarrassed. He turned to Licole, angry. "Licole, did you start the damn saw today?" Yes, she had checked the saw in the morning; that was her job, the same way that Ramon checks the saw in the morning. She grabbed the K-12 and started it herself. The saw worked just fine. "People say that you don't have to prove yourself," she tells me, "but you do."

One guy had a habit of always slamming the door in her face. He was rude to her, nasty, and for no reason she could understand. Finally she pulled the guy aside and asked him point-blank, "Why are you being such an asshole?"

"I don't want people to think that I like you," he said.

Licole says this was not uncommon: guys afraid of getting in trouble and being rude just to prove that they *didn't* like her in an inappropriate way.

Another potential issue for women firefighters: Licole cautions that "whoever you date, they have to be very strong and very secure." Not every guy, she says, can handle the threat of a woman spending so much time with male firefighters. The bonding with firefighters is real. Those twenty-four-hour shifts are spent not just working but also laughing, bullshitting, and sharing traumatic experiences ("A guy raped Tiara and killed her") that a non-firefighter—even a spouse—can never fully understand. Even though the time Licole spends with male firefighters is innocent, she says it can be tough for some boyfriends to handle. And she doesn't state the obvious: that these male firefighters are tough, strong, and physically imposing—an insecure boyfriend's nightmare.

Licole doesn't like to make a fuss over gender issues, but says "I won't be bullied or harassed," and she once filed an official gender discrimination case—and won. She also told me that "If a woman, minority, or *anyone* feels bullied, harassed sexually or otherwise, or discriminated against, they have a right to say something, and it's okay to say something. It's going to be a long uphill and lonely battle, but it will help someone else in the future."

Most of these incidents happened years ago, and the worst of it twenty years ago. Licole stresses that the culture has improved dramatically. "People seem more open to the idea that this can be a place for women," she says, adding that she now feels well respected. "I have absolutely no problems now," she says. "None."

Why aren't there more women in the fire service? That continues to be debated. "I don't think many women are interested in the job," suggests Battalion Chief Derrick Phillips, who's in charge of the department's training. "It's a dirty job. You spend a lot of time away from home." He says that he has seen many women finish near the top of the testing list, but when their number comes up, they decline to join. As for the fire chief, Jenkerson says that he is gender-blind: he's happy to have any firefighter, male or female, who can pass the test and do the job.

This goes to the crux of the gender controversy: the test. Historically, the rationale for the lack of female firefighters is that not as many women are physically able to pass the test. Which begs the question: Is the test itself fair?

Many firefighters, especially older male firefighters, argue that testing standards should never be lowered just to include more women, and doing so would compromise the fire service and put lives at risk. It's a compelling argument. And it's something that Baltimore fire captain Angela Hughes, president of Women in Fire, agrees with. "The standards should not be lowered. Absolutely not," she tells me, and then adds, "But what kind of standards are you setting?"

Hughes says that the physical standards of the test should match the requirements of the job. As a thought experiment: Imagine that a bank gives a test for everyone who wants to be a banker. Now imagine that the bank asks all of the applicants—regardless of gender, because they're "gender-blind"—to do as many push-ups as they can. And if the aspiring banker can't squeeze out one hundred push-ups, then they won't be hired. Clearly this would unfairly punish women, who tend to do fewer push-ups, and clearly this would be discriminatory, and clearly this would be illegal, because the job of a banker has very little to do with push-ups.

But extend this logic to the fire service. Yes, a firefighter needs to be strong. No one questions this. They need to throw ladders, run with hose, carry a body up a flight of stairs. Lives are at stake. But maybe doing one hundred push-ups isn't the best way to measure those skills. Men tend to have more upper-body strength. Women use the strength in their legs. "So, to throw a ladder, a man might use his arms," says Hughes. "I might use my shoulders and legs, and throw my ass into it."

I run this by Chief Phillips, the head of training, who says he agrees 100 percent. He hates the old tests of brute force. "That's just some arbitrary bullshit," he says, adding that those tests could be a way of keeping women down. The courts have largely agreed, tossing out tests that have been found to be discriminatory. As Federal Judge Charles Sifton wrote in 1982, "What must be identified are not those who are strongest or fastest, but instead those who . . . can perform the punishing tasks of firefighting as they are actually required to be performed."

Phillips says that the design of the St. Louis test comes from an evaluation of job functions, not a measure of raw strength. "You won't find anyone doing one hundred sit-ups here. That's police academy shit."

Yet there are more subtle forms of bias. Corinne Bendersky, a professor at UCLA Anderson School of Management, studies gender bias in the firefighting service. As part of her research, she found that captains are more likely to excessively drill female firefighters on physically grueling tasks, going well beyond the reasonable training that's given to men. She cites a clear example: the two-person throw of a thirty-five-foot ladder. This is a ladder that can weigh 129 pounds. It's a monster. In almost every real-world scenario, throwing this ladder is a job for three firefighters, but in extraordinarily rare cases in the field, you might need to do it with two. "Women firefighters say that they get drilled repeatedly and excessively" on a two-firefighter throw of the thirty-five-foot ladder, Corrine tells me, "even though they would never do that in the field. This is very clear evidence to me of bias."

Again I run this by Phillips, who essentially agrees, and says that the St. Louis Fire Department trains in the thirty-five-foot ladder throw with three firefighters, not two. "It's a three-man raise; it's a heavy fucking ladder," he says. "If you take a smaller guy and make him throw the ladder ten times in a row, I bet he can't do it, either."

Licole's advice to a woman considering joining the fire service? On the one hand she says, "Pray on it. It's not for everybody." She points out that it's not for you if you don't like hard work and if you're not into serving people—a common refrain. "But," she adds, "once you look into your inner being, and realize it's something you really want to do, I would say do it." Licole notes that, for women, the option of a career in firefighting is "one of the best-kept secrets." When she grew up, no one told her it was even on the table. Now she can't envision her life without it: "I would tell any young woman [who wants to do it] 'Get your medic license and become a firefighter.' I really would."

Bonus? Licole appreciates that she can be a positive role model, especially for little girls. When she's on the fire truck, she loves it when little girls see her—a woman firefighter!—and then smile. "They just smile so big and wave like crazy," Licole says. And then the girls want the firefighters to honk the horn. "And then we'll honk our horn, and they scream, because it scares the shit out of them."

GIVEN THE FIRE SERVICE'S struggle with inclusivity, I'm eager to speak with a firefighter at Engine House 8, a twenty-five-year-old rookie named Cody Carpenter: white, six feet tall, with tattoos on both forearms. Cody entered the St. Louis Fire Academy in the same class as Ramon, and the two of them get along well. "He's solid as fuck," Cody says of Ramon. "He's a good dude."

Growing up in Illinois, Cody wanted to be a firefighter at

age five. He was inspired by his grandfather, a firefighter with forty-three years of service, and at age thirteen he became an "explorer" firefighter (a junior firefighter at a volunteer department); at sixteen he took EMT classes while still in high school; by eighteen he was a volunteer firefighter; and by twenty-one he had his paramedic's license.

Cody longed to be a career firefighter somewhere, anywhere, so he took thirty different tests across Georgia, Indiana, Illinois, and Missouri. This is yet another path to becoming a firefighter: a shotgun approach where you take loads of tests and you hope that, eventually, a spot will open up somewhere. First he was hired at a department in Illinois and then, finally, his number came up at his top choice: St. Louis.

Now Cody is a firefighter at Engine House 8. "This is the fire department you dream of as a kid," he says. "You walk in here and see guys around the kitchen table drinking coffee, bullshitting with each other. You walk into the engine bay, and it still smells like a house fire." Cody might be the most upbeat firefighter I've met.

When Cody was sixteen, while enrolled at a Christian high school, he came out as gay. The school threatened to expel him, so he was forced back into the closet until he graduated. His grandfather—the same grandfather who had inspired him to become a firefighter—refused to speak to him for years.

At age eighteen, while still in Illinois, he came out to his firefighter buddies. "It wasn't a big deal," he tells me. One night when hanging out, they asked him, "Hey, where's your girlfriend? Bring your girlfriend out!" Cody told them, laughing a bit, "I like dudes, guys!" As Cody remembers it, they said, "Oh, no fucking shit, man! Oh my god! We're so sorry!" It was never an issue, he says, adding that "nobody's ever treated me differently."

And as for coming out in St. Louis? At the fire academy, after all of that intense training with Ramon and his fellow recruits—the ten tens, the burpees, the sprints up the tower in bunker gear—Cody didn't feel that he *needed* to tell them he was gay, but because they were his genuine friends, why not? He forgets how it came up. But on a rare night off from the academy, at a bar, he told them and they said, as Cody remembers it, "Dude, that's so cool. Who the fuck cares?"

There isn't solid data on how many openly gay firefighters are in the fire service, but the percentage—whatever it is—feels absurdly low. Roughly one in twenty adults (4.5 percent) in the United States identifies as LGBT, according to a 2017 Gallup poll, yet the percentage of openly LGBT firefighters is almost certainly closer to zero percent than 4.5 percent. When I asked Mosby, the gregarious and capable communications officer who knows just about everyone, if I could speak to an openly gay firefighter—and there are nearly six hundred firefighters in St. Louis—he paused, considered this, and said, "Let me get back to you."

Given the old-school, "screw political correctness" attitude of many firefighters, I had—perhaps revealing my own biases—assumed that the firehouse would be a rough place for an openly gay person to work. Cody insists that's not the case, at least for him, and that almost everyone has been "totally chill." After he graduated the academy, when he first arrived at Engine House 8, he guessed that his new squad mates had heard through the rumor mill that he was gay, but he didn't bring it up at first. He just focused on doing his job and doing it well. They didn't haze him. "I was never treated differently. I did the shit work, because I was the newest guy, but they never fucked with me."

After Cody had been on the track for a few months, one day at lunch, he told the other firefighters, "Hey, I know you guys know I'm gay."

"It's okay! It's okay! It's okay!" they said.

"You guys are so chill, I didn't think it'd be a problem," Cody said.

"It's not!"

And in true firefighter fashion, they decided to fuck with their captain. (The captain hadn't been part of the lunch conversation.) Cody bought a pack of Skittles, and he also bought a condolence card. He gave the captain the Skittles and the card, which said, "I'm sorry you have to work with a gay guy." When the captain opened the card he cracked up laughing. "Hey, man, we don't give a fuck," he said. "It don't matter to us."

It's hard to tell if Cody's experience is the norm or an exception, given the striking lack of openly gay firefighters. And in some firehouses in St. Louis, you can still catch the whiff of the occasional gay joke. When pressed, Cody clarifies that "I don't think that the bigots are gone, or that the people who want to gay bash are gone" but says that if they exist, they keep it to themselves.

When I asked Jenkerson why he thinks there aren't more openly gay firefighters, he says that he'd be happy to have more, but adds that the department doesn't "do any particular outreach to any one particular group of people." Jenkerson does walk in the Pride Parade. And he notes that he knew a couple of openly gay firefighters in the 1980s, that they were "tough, tough guys," and that it "wasn't any big deal."

Cody's advice for someone who is gay and wants to become a firefighter? It boils down to this: Do the work. Get good. Then (maybe) share.

"It's just like any job," he says. "You don't walk into somewhere and pretend that you own the place." He says that when you're first breaking into a crew, no one wants to know about your personal life. First you cut your teeth. "You can't just walk in somewhere and be, like, 'I like dudes. Tough luck if you don't like it.' Walk in. Show them that you know how to do your job. Become their friend. Give them a reason to like you. Give them a reason to keep you on their crew and say, 'Hey, we got the best new prick in the city.'"

Once that trust is earned, Cody says, the crew will want to learn about your family, your hobbies, your dating life. "For a young gay person, it truly has nothing to do with you being gay," he says. "It has everything to do with you being a human, and a decent human, first. A good firefighter, a good toilet scrubber. You have to humble yourself every day in this job. Our job is to serve people." (Again that word: "serve." It's in every firefighter's bones.)

"I love fighting fires," Cody tells me. "I don't want anybody's house to be on fire . . . but if there is going to be a fire, I want to be there." He loves going on medical calls, and likes to use them as an opportunity to size up the buildings in his district. "If you go on a medical call and hear a chirping battery in the smoke detector, that's a chance to replace the alarm," he says.

Cody notes that most people—non-firefighters—complain about their jobs and say things like "I have to go to work today." For him it's different. "I *get* to go to fucking work today! I get to spend time with some of my favorite people in the world, and I get to do some pretty fucking cool shit, and I get paid for it."

## PTSD

5:00 P.M.

For most of America, this would be the end of the workday and time to crack a beer. Yet firefighters are less than halfway through their twenty-four-hour shifts. The sun is still bright in the long July day. Richter and I are back in his SUV. He smokes a cigarette and listens to the department radio, which has brought him surprisingly little action today. He turns to me. "You know what you are, my friend? You're a white cloud."

A white cloud is something of a jinx, a guarantee that you won't see any fires. Of course this is good news for the people whose homes are not burning, but it's bad news for those who are eager to fight fires. "We're fire hungry," Ramon told me earlier, an honest-to-God gleam in his eyes. Richter tells me that white clouds can take the form of a journalist, a book author, or a TV news crew—civilians who tag along with firefighters in the hopes of seeing a dramatic fire—but then nothing happens and they don't "get" to watch a family's life get ruined.

As we pass yet another stretch of broken buildings, Richter perks up. "Holy shit," he says. "It's a miracle!" He points to a vacant lot. He's surprised and pleased to see that some of these doomed buildings have been demolished, thanks to a donation from Jack Dorsey. The Twitter CEO is a native of St. Louis and has ambitions of jump-starting the city into an innovation hub. Dorsey's side-gig company, Square, employs five hundred tech workers in the Central West End, and he has announced plans to hire nine hundred more.

With no fires in sight, Richter's en route to one of his four firehouses, where the firefighters have just taken a class about coping with trauma. He's curious to learn if the class was worthwhile, or what he calls "let-me-hold-your-hand-and-give-you-a-group-hug bullshit." Richter clarifies that if a firefighter needs help, they should absolutely get that help. But, like many old-timers, he's skeptical of what he considers "'Kumbaya' therapy," or people "blowing smoke up your ass and telling you it will all be okay. It won't. Deal with it."

We pull up to the engine house, Richter lights a cigarette, and before he can ask about the trauma class, the firefighters tell him about an old lady who keeps dialing 911—another frequent flyer.

"Eighteen calls in the last eleven days, Chief," says one of the firefighters, a woman. She says that most of the calls come in the dead of night. One night the old lady called 911 five times, and each time, as always, the firefighters responded as fast as they could. Then the old lady would ask them to help with errands or maybe bring her cookies or a soda. "She says that she's falling out of bed, but I think she's putting herself on the floor because she wants the attention," the firefighter says. "She's abusing the system."

"She's not abusing the system, she's *using* the system," says Richter. "She just needs more resources." Richter guesses that the old lady, imagining herself out of options, does the only thing she can think of: dial 911. The episode now commands his full attention. He jots down the woman's name, then immediately hops on the phone to try and see what can be done, such as transferring her to a nursing home.

Once he's off the phone, the firefighters debrief Richter. They liked the class that explained how to spot the signs of PTSD—irritability, low morale, depression, going through the motions, a change in attitude—and encouraged an open discussion of trauma. The class also touched on "vicarious trauma," the idea that your teammates' horrors can, over time, impact you as well. "The fire service is made up of this old-school mentality of 'Suck it up,'" the female firefighter tells me. "A young person puts on that facade and inherits the stoicism. But you shouldn't be afraid of saying, 'Man, I just saw these kids decapitated, and it affected me.'"

Richter nods and tries to be supportive, but he doesn't hide the fact that he is very much a part of the "Suck it up" generation. He looks at the younger firefighters and says in his deep, gravelly voice, with a hint of a smile, "I will try and be more compassionate."

The fire service, nationwide, is trying to be more compassionate. Especially in the wake of 9/11, the fire service has grappled with how to better acknowledge the realities of PTSD, how to remove the stigma, and how to provide better resources. Many need these resources. One study found that 143 firefighters committed suicide in 2015—more deaths by suicide than in the line of duty. And the actual number could be higher, as the Firefighter Behavioral Health Alliance estimates that only 40 percent of suicides are reported.

Captain Frank Leto, a thirty-two-year veteran firefighter, is the director of the New York City Fire Department's counseling unit. He is one of the hundreds of firefighters who raced to Ground Zero on 9/11. This is still a raw, sensitive subject for many firefighters—particularly FDNY firefighters—but Frank shares what it was like, on the darkest day of the fire service's history, to serve on September 11. Frank, along with so many grieving firefighters, dug through the mountain of smoking debris. For days and weeks they searched the pile of ash; first they searched for survivors; then they searched for bodies. They didn't stop to sleep. They barely ate. Frank's depleted body told him to stop, but he couldn't. The firefighters picked up chunks of debris, they evaluated it, and they smelled it to see if it was human. There were so many deaths that the FDNY needed to issue emergency promotions to restore the ranks.

Frank worked on that pile of bones and bricks and ash for days, weeks, months. He felt isolated from the rest of the world. He remembers one of the first social events he forced himself to attend: a Super Bowl party in February, almost five months after 9/11, to watch the Patriots play the Rams. He walked in the room and it was disorienting to see that kind of *normalcy* among the non-firefighters. "I walked in, and life had gone on for them," Frank tells me. "They weren't talking about the body parts they had recovered, or losing their son.

They were talking about the Super Bowl. Their life had gone on. My life had not. For me it was still September twelfth. For them it was February 2002."

In the wake of 9/11, Frank devoted himself to providing resources for firefighters coping with trauma. He says that across the fire service, there's a growing awareness that a healthy department requires a strong behavioral health program, and that it needs to be more than just a token. "Not only do you need to take care of your rigs and make sure the equipment is shiny and well-oiled, but make sure your men and women are taken care of," he says, adding that PTSD should be taken "just as seriously as a broken ankle."

How common is PTSD? Some studies say it affects between 8 percent and 30 percent of firefighters. "I would venture to say it's not that high," says Frank. "Or I would say it's on the lower end of what the researches are saying."

We tend to think that firefighter PTSD is caused by a single trauma, like the death of a small child. Yet, more often than not, Frank says, it's caused by a series of traumatic events. This is something that researcher Sara Anne Jahnke, of the National Development and Research Institutes, has called repeated exposure to trauma, or RET. After all of the cumulative horror you witness, maybe you go on one more awful call, and this is the straw that breaks the camel's back. "Maybe you look at another deformed human body, and it just hits you," says Frank. "You've seen it thirty times before, and you don't know why, but this one got you."

Frank says that you get back from the call, you return to the firehouse and go about your normal routine: you clean, cook, eat. "And then you get into your car, [and you're] at a stoplight, and the tears are running down your cheek," he says. "It just comes out. And that's okay. It's a healthy response. We're not machines. We're not robots."

He has one more message for current and future fire-fighters: "I would encourage them to be part of the solution by stepping forward when they are having a difficult time and talking about their recovery from difficult times." The mere act of talking about trauma, says Frank, can help others who are dealing with similar issues. "You talking about your experience can save someone's life," he says, noting that the dream of every firefighter is to charge into a burning building and save someone's life. "You have that opportunity every day in a firehouse: where you can save someone's life just by talking about your experience."

## "Odd, Odd Stuff"

Jenkerson tells me that when a good firefighter walks up to a fire, their mind cycles through a database of files. Jenkerson calls this a recognition-primed decision (RPD) model.

"Your mind is a big collection of files," Jenkerson tells me as we're sitting in his office. "If I ask you 'What's the first car you drove?' an image comes to your mind, right?"

"Right."

He gives more examples: the first time you kissed a girl and the first time you lost a friend. Your mind stores all of these files. Using the RPD model, a veteran chief looks at a fire and the first one hundred decisions are automatic. A quick glance tells him that he has a two-story, two-family brick building, there are kids upstairs, those wires will cause a problem, the roof has asphalt tiles, the nearest hydrant is two hundred yards away, there are two chimneys, and on and on. After those first one hundred automatic decisions, he notices that—wait—the smoke is darker than it should be. Something's not right. The best firefighters, Jenkerson says, "pick up on these things, and that comes with repetitive actions and repetitive scenarios that they've seen. And they can't teach that in a book."

As firefighters advance in their careers, the scope of those files expands to include the issues Jenkerson has been juggling all afternoon: PTSD awareness, cancer initiatives, the annual budget, arson investigations. And he's still dealing with that damn shortage of paramedics. He responds to the dreaded Insurance Services Office (ISO) audit: a once-a-decade assessment of the fire department for which he must furnish paperwork showing that, for example, each of the 18,000 fire hydrants in St. Louis have been recently turned on and checked. For a fire chief, the ISO audit is a yearlong root canal.

Then he pokes his head in the fire investigation unit's office to get a rundown on potential arsons. St. Louis gets between fifteen and seventeen fires a day: building fires, car fires, and dumpster fires. Jenkerson sits with the chief fire investigator to review the fires and try to spot patterns. Usually there are none, but a few years ago they noticed a cluster of house fires that all seemed to happen around the same time of day. When they plotted them on a map, they realized all of the fires occurred along one bus line, and they matched the times of each fire to a bus schedule. They caught the guy.

Jenkerson also has to deal with the literal heat, i.e., the weather. July is brutal. It causes strokes, especially among the elderly. So Jenkerson partners with an organization called Cool Down St. Louis to distribute air conditioners to elderly residents for free and then sends firefighters to install them. The *Today* show dropped by to spotlight the initiative.

Fire chiefs are always worried about injuries, so Jenkerson hunts for the root causes of on-site accidents. After poring through the department's injury reports, his team realized that torn rotator cuffs and shoulder damage accounted for a disproportionate number of firefighters' injuries.

That's why they redesigned the fire truck. Jenkerson's team whipped up plans for storing ladders and hoses waist-high, to make it more ergonomically friendly to deploy them. "We wanted to design it so that a firefighter never has to climb on top of the truck," he says. They showed the drawings to a truck manufacturer and asked, "Can you build that?" The manufacturer said no. So they found a different manufacturer, who eventually built them a new fire truck to their specifications. Jenkerson showed the truck off at a firefighter's conference in Indianapolis. Engineers and firefighters examined it, amazed.

Then there are the wild cards. Only 7.4 percent of the St. Louis Fire Department's calls are for fires, which is double the national average of 3.8 percent. More often than not, the fire department is a catch-all for emergencies, as in the winter of 1982, when a once-in-a-century blizzard shut St. Louis down for a week. Shops, roads, restaurants, and schools were all closed. The only thing working was the fire department. Jenkerson's squad flew all over, doing things like delivering prescriptions door-to-door, picking up doctors and bringing them to the hospital, and chopping down five-foot icicles that hung from skyscrapers and could fall and kill people. There were a million things like this—"just weird things," Jenkerson says. "Just odd, odd stuff."

Much of this "odd, odd stuff" is handled by the rescue squads, including the one led by "Super Mario," Captain Mario Montero. This elite unit flies across the city for out-of-the-ordinary emergencies like amphibious rescues, releasing people trapped in elevators, or extracting victims from the rubble of collapsed buildings. These firefighters are specialists. They don't get dispatched to commercial fire alarms or most EMS calls. They ride in a gleaming red 56,000-pound beast of a truck loaded with a dazzling range of tools that would make Batman envious, including bulletproof vests (used during the Ferguson protests), eight saws (not including handsaws), a jackhammer (in case a building collapses), portable generators, and an inflatable speedboat.

Mario, forty-five, is Cuban American. His parents brought him to the United States when he was a kid. He's tall, wears a light blue captain's shirt, and has a crisp mustache. He takes pride in his appearance. "Rescue squad should be at a higher level," he says of the dress code.

The guys at Squad 1 have been with each other for years, which reflects a striking feature of the fire service: turnover is low. Transfers to other departments are rare. If you move, you must *start all over again*. Let's say that as your first job as a firefighter you get hired by the department in El Paso, Texas. Then you get married. Thirteen years later your spouse gets a dream job in Chicago, and you have to move. In Chicago you will need to retest and start from scratch. Maybe you do this if you've only been on the track for two years, but if you're closer to your pension, which begins at year 20, your original department holds a strong pull.

Like Chief Richter, Mario sees the worst of the worst. Squad 1 goes on missions that are optimistically called "amphibious rescues," but, more often than not, those are grim expeditions to recover a body. They'll find corpses, or "floaters," the skin pale and bloated and stinking of rot. They see bodies festooned with maggots. Mario once found a twelve-year-old girl sitting on a sofa, perfectly still, and thought she was in shock. Then he looked closer. The girl had a bullet in her skull.

Then there are missions like the one in 2014, when Squad 1 was dispatched to the Eads Bridge, the oldest bridge on the Mississippi River. The bridge is one of the city's most Instagrammed landmarks; in 1873, when it was nearing completion, the *New York Times* called it "the World's Eighth Wonder." It's also a favorite spot for suicide jumpers. On this night, a young woman climbed onto the bridge and then went even higher, scaling a steel tower that held power lines. She threatened to jump.

The police arrived first. Yet the cops didn't have the gear or the training required to climb up the tower and attempt a rescue. Enter Squad 1. The truck raced across the bridge to where the jumper had climbed. Mario grabbed his rope gear. His rappelling credentials are so well burnished that once, for the annual Guns 'N Hoses charity boxing event in full bunker gear he rappelled from the ceiling of the arena into the boxing ring, a dramatic entrance straight from the WWE's playbook.

Along with another firefighter, Mario began climbing up the steel tower like Spider-Man. He didn't use a safety harness. He could have, but that would have slowed him down. *What if she jumps while I'm making myself safer?* This is one of the countless split-second calculations that firefighters make on every call, and they almost always prioritize the safety of the victim—a complete stranger—over their own.

As Mario climbed the tower, the jumper spotted him from above. She began screaming. A young African American woman, maybe in her early twenties, she was not happy to see Mario. "Don't come near me!" she yelled. A second later she added, "I hate men!"

Firefighters have many roles. Now Mario had to play the part of therapist. He guessed that she and her boyfriend or husband were in some kind of dispute and now she was angry at the world. She stood on a tiny ledge jumping up and down. Mario worried that even if she *didn't* intend to jump, she might fall over the edge by accident. A fall from that height meant certain death. Another body. So many bodies . . .

When Mario reached the top, he stood on the opposite side of the twelve-foot-by-twelve-foot platform, so as not to encroach or threaten the woman. "Don't come near me!" she yelled. "I don't want you touching me!"

He told her that he was there only to help her. He promised that he wouldn't touch her. "I just want to keep you safe."

"I want to kill myself," she said, and jumped up and down again. "I'm going to kill myself!"

On the ground far below, where the people looked like tiny dots, a crowd gathered; it included police, firefighters, the woman's family, and an official negotiator who had been summoned to the scene. The woman kept repeating that she would kill herself. She kept jumping up and down.

"I don't want you touching me!" she said again, tears on her face.

Mario kept his voice level, soothing. "I promise we won't touch you."

The woman said that she was worried she would go to jail. Through a phone, Mario conveyed this to the negotiator below. "Reassure her that she's not going to jail," said the negotiator, so Mario passed that along. "You have my word," he said. He told her that there were people she could talk to and that killing herself was not the solution. He stayed calm.

Something he said must have clicked. She agreed to climb down, but insisted that she do so on her own.

Another tricky call. If Mario insisted on carrying her, she might jump. If he let her climb herself, she might fall. "No problem," he told her. "But I'm going to need you to slip on this rope harness." Mario had quickly fashioned an emergency rope harness—yet another file in a firefighter's database. Doing his best not to touch her, Mario guided her through the process of putting on the rope harness. He slid the rope through a carabiner. Secured the rope to the tower. *Click*.

They began climbing down, with Mario keeping the woman between himself and another firefighter, just in case something weird happened.

Something weird happened.

Halfway down, the woman changed her mind. She wanted to jump after all.

She began to climb back to the ledge, where this time, for real, she would try to throw herself to her death. All she had to do was unhook the rope from the carabiner.

*Shit, shit, shit*, Mario thought.

But his fail-safe worked. Because she was sandwiched between the two firefighters, they blocked her from going back up. Finally, as the crowd below let out a collective sigh, they reached the bottom of the tower.

In acknowledgment of the rescue, Mario and the other firefighter, Tom Moore, were given a Heroism Award from

*Firehouse* magazine. Mario was never thanked by the woman or by the family. "It's not about that, for us," Mario tells me.

And he doesn't know what happened to the woman. Again, firefighters almost never do.

## "Lemme Give You a Hand"

5:30 P.M.

Battalion Chief Richter's next call is for a vehicle accident, but the twist is that the accident involves a fire truck—one of his own. It's only a fender bender. When we get to the scene, it appears that the truck, while making a wide left turn, nicked a concrete median. No one was hurt. Nothing looks damaged. Yet, paperwork being paperwork, the chief is summoned to supervise the incident report.

When the chief arrives, he doesn't need to say anything. He doesn't chew anyone out. The sheer gravity of his presence—his frown, like that of a stern father; the crew cut, the hard eyes, the swaggering mustache—is its own rebuke. He inspects the minor damage to the side of the truck, where a long red panel now curves in like a parenthesis. "Goddammit," he mutters. He tells me that it's not a big deal. "It's city property versus city property," so there's no need to gum the system with red tape. He fills out an accident report.

Richter's crew views him with a mix of respect, love,

and fear. That likely began in the winter of 2007, when he took over as battalion chief. On his first day he supervised the response to a two-alarm fire. "I saw so many firefighters doing stupid things," he remembers. He watched, horrified, as one firefighter used a chain saw to slice open a window . . . and then left the chain saw running on the ground, where it slid across the ice and hit the fire engine. He watched as a firefighter took off a plexiglass window and put it on the ice, where it slid dangerously, because, as Richter puts it, plexiglass is "slick as shit, the best sled ever." He watched as firefighters fell into an open stairwell.

"If I wasn't so stressed, I'd be laughing my ass off," he says.

Richter vowed to clean up the district. "I turned my pea brain into management mode," he says, and gathered his captains, issuing them a new set of expectations. "Nothing earth-shattering," he explains. "Just keep your fucking head out of your ass and do what you're supposed to do." He shows me a document that he gave his crew, a pithy two-page memo that includes edicts like "Train like your life depends on it—cause it does," "After the fire . . . help occupants as much as we can . . . save the high fives for the engine house," and "Do the basics well." Now Richter's district is widely regarded as one of the finest in the department. "I'm pretty demanding," he confesses.

Ten or twenty years from now, a firefighter may be certain

to avoid a fender bender like the one Richter just supervised, because the fire trucks will likely drive themselves. "We'll have autonomous driving fire trucks by the year 2040," predicts Gary Ludwig, the president of the International Association of Fire Chiefs and fire chief for Champaign, Illinois.

Here's how Ludwig envisions the future of firefighting tech:

A drone is instantly dispatched to the scene and hovers over or inside the burning building, feeding you real-time data that you can analyze while riding in the truck. The size-up can happen before you even arrive. When you're inside the burning building and have zero visibility, your mask will have a display (à la Google Glass) that gives you digital bread crumbs to help you find your way around, and lets you see through the smoke with a built-in thermal-imaging camera. Body vests monitor the crew's vitals. That data zooms back to the battalion chief, who will then know if a firefighter is at risk and needs to be pulled from the fire. Meanwhile, the chief will look at a 3-D schematic of the building and know the precise location of every firefighter.

"These are all things I know that are coming," says Ludwig.

Richter finishes with the accident report. We get back in his red SUV. As we're pulling away, he spots a car that's pulled over to the side of the road. A few guys start to push the car; looks like it needs a jump.

"Lemme give you a hand," the chief hollers. He gets out of the SUV, jogs over to the car, and helps these strangers push their car.

This is classic Richter and very much on-brand for the fire service. Firefighters are helpers. Doers. Problem solvers. They don't judge or discriminate. Earlier today a homeless guy asked Richter for a cigarette, and the chief immediately obliged. They smoked together, side by side, in comfortable silence as if they were friends. Later, after dinner, the chief will be the first to spring from the table and clean dishes.

Optics matter. Maintaining a good public image is part of a battalion chief's role. "I'm driving around in a billboard," Richter says, referring to his bright red SUV emblazoned with the STLFD logo. "I could be the only impression that people see of the fire department." On the front of every firehouse in St. Louis is a yellow sign that says "Safe Place," a collaboration with the nonprofit organization Youth in Need. In one of Richter's houses, I watched as two young boys, maybe aged three and eight, African American, shuffled into the engine bay. A firefighter gave the youngest one a hug. "How you doing? Let me see those stitches of yours?" The firefighter pulled out his wallet and grabbed a dollar so they could buy a can of soda. The kids are regulars and they often swing by to climb on the truck and play in the station. "The dads aren't in the picture," the firefighter told me.

In the winter Richter instructs his firefighters to buy used bikes on Craigslist, fix them up, and then give them to needy kids for Christmas. He knows they don't have much. "There's not a lot of opportunity in life when your toy is a smashed aluminum can and you're kicking it back and forth on the street," he says.

Richter looks out the window. Once more we pass some broken buildings that have burned before and will burn again. The chief, this bear of a man, says softly, and almost too quietly for me to hear, "It's heartbreaking."

## III

## Night

## The Great Turtle Fire

6:00 P.M.

There's a children's book called *A Day in the Life of a Fire-fighter*, by Linda Hayward. In the section on dinner, firefighters politely chat about a fishing trip. The meal is sweet and G-rated.

Here's the adult version:

In one of the firehouses I visit (which I'll keep anonymous here for obvious reasons), a firefighter cooks dinner. He cuts the fat from the chicken, coats it with marinade, chops the broccoli, then peels and slices the potatoes. While he's seasoning the veggies, another firefighter tells him in a booming voice, "I thought I had penile cancer! My dick was so raw . . . I was on WebMD and shit, looking up penile cancer."

"So what happened?" the cook asks, stirring the broccoli.

"It wasn't penile cancer," he says. "It's just that she was working me hard. Too much fucking."

I can't help myself: "Is this someone you met at a bar?"

"Nah. My wife."

The firehouse is not just an office, a workplace. The firehouse is its own universe with its own language, which outsiders will find raw. "Firemen live in a world apart from other civilians. The rest of the world seems to change, but the firehouses do not," writes David Halberstam in his masterpiece 9/11 FDNY profile, *Firehouse*. "This is, in fact, as close to a hermetically sealed world as you are likely to find in contemporary America."

In Ramon's firehouse, we eat dinner quickly—firefighters eat fast—and the guys have an easy rapport. Lots of inside jokes and banter, the kind you only get through spending all your time together in a confined space. They don't haze, but they delight in giving each other shit. "I fuck with Calvin [another firefighter] all the time for being overweight," says Willy, explaining that "if we're not messing with you, it means we don't like you." Then he gives Ramon a look and says, deadpan, "But with Ramon it's different. We mess with you because we don't like you."

If you can't take a joke, you're going to have a tough time. Richter once had a captain who was precious about his day planner—he *hated* when people touched that beloved day planner—so they would steal and hide it. One day they hung the planner from a flagpole; one day they covered it with shrink wrap; one day they cooked it into a meatloaf.

The pranks can be vicious. When Richter was a new prick in the 1980s, the turnout gear came with long boots that went to your hips, and you pulled them up with handles. You set your boots next to the truck, and when you caught a fire, you jumped into the boots. (Many firefighters still leave their boots next to the fire truck, at the ready.)

So when Richter, the new prick, went on a call, someone had zip-tied the heels of his boots together. He tried to pull up the boots: no dice. The truck was about to leave. Shit! So he hopped up on the truck awkwardly, like a rabbit, with his heels still tied. "The whole way there I'm in a fucking panic," he tells me. The gag didn't end there. When Richter arrived, he lifted his helmet from the engine and was hit in the face by a ball of confetti, which the guys had jerry-rigged as a fun surprise. "I was already freaking out, and that gave me a full-blown heart attack."

As battalion chief, he supervised a fire at the corner of Temple and Ridge Streets. After his crew had snuffed out the fire—but with the building still smoking—the woman who lived in the house, distraught, told Richter that she had left something important inside: her turtles.

He ordered a probie, who was small and nervous: "Go inside and get those turtles."

The probie was in a near panic. Probies don't usually speak directly to the battalion chief, and Richter could be terrifying. The probie sprinted back into the building—*There are lives at stake!*—and soon emerged with a turtle in each hand.

Richter turned to the woman. "Ma'am, is that all of the turtles?"

"No, there are two more!" the woman cried.

Richter barked to the probie: "Go back in there and get the rest of the turtles!"

The probie charged back into the house as if he were saving a baby, and soon found the other turtles. Once outside, he nearly collapsed in exhaustion.

Richter later wrote up a faux letter of commendation: "Firefighter rescued four turtles from the Great Turtle Fire of Temple and Ridge."

IN THE PRODUCE SECTION of Schnucks supermarket, there's a sign that says "We consider you family." The sign is a bit much, because it's obviously not true. I'm a customer, not family. People use the phrase "We're one big family" so often that it's a cliché, from grocery stores to banks to Vin Diesel in *The Fast and the Furious*.

Yet with firefighters it's not a cliché. It's legit. The family bond is authentic, and every firefighter stressed the importance of this brother and sisterhood.

"No matter where you are in your life, as long as you've got a good crew, they've got your back," says one firefighter during dinner. "When I went through my divorce—and I had a pretty fucked-up divorce—having these guys around helped reassure me." Stories like this are everywhere. If you're sick, one phone call will rally a crew of firefighters to bring medicine, cook food, clean your gutters. Richter once had surgery that took him out of action. From his bed he heard a lawn mower, peered out the front window, and saw a firefighter cutting his grass. "There's all kinds of shit like that," he says. "Somebody's car breaks down, you go pick them up on the highway. Somebody's car breaks down in Illinois, you go pick them up." This is what they do.

The flip side is that you spend less time with your actual family. As a firefighter, you might miss the first time your child loses a tooth, or the family dinner on Sunday night, or your kid waiting up for Santa Claus. "It takes a toll on your family," Jenkerson acknowledges. "Even if you have the perfect family. They'll ask, 'Can't you get off for Christmas Eve?'"

## Race[*]

6:30 P.M.

It's burger night at Engine House 33. Licole and the rest of the firefighters and medics, all male, mostly African American, are engaged in the same relaxed banter I've heard everywhere else in the department. One of the firefighters, Billy, has been in this engine house since 1993. They give each other shit while polishing off the burgers. One of them is short, has ripped muscles, and wears an extra-tight shirt. They call him "Lil Swole" and he bursts out laughing.

At Ramon's firehouse, two black firefighters share dinner with two white firefighters. And in Richter's engine house, equally diverse, the large crew wolfs down breaded pork chops coated with a spicy Cajun seasoning.

On the surface, these dinners—and the overall department—look like a model of congenial and "color-blind" race relations. Yet the St. Louis Fire Department, like the city overall and the nation at large, has a troubled, complicated, and at times brutal history of racial injustice. What's more, St. Louis borders Ferguson, which is so close that you can drive there from the Gateway Arch in under seventeen minutes.

---

[*] Note: This book was written before the protests stemming from the killing of George Floyd.

During the Ferguson protests, the St. Louis Fire Department was not in command of the fire response—that was the Ferguson Fire Department—but they watched, learned, took notes, and prepared themselves in case something similar cropped up.

Then came the Stockley case. The setup was similar to Ferguson: Jason Stockley, a white St. Louis police officer, shot and killed a young African American man, Anthony Lamar Smith, after the cop was recorded saying, during a car chase, "Going to kill this motherfucker, don't you know it." In September of 2017, a jury found the cop innocent of murder. Just as in Ferguson, outraged citizens gathered to demonstrate.

Enter the fire department.

"This was our first real test of homeland security," Jenkerson tells me, once again in his office. In the wake of 9/11 the fire service has expanded responsibilities for antiterrorism and homeland security. This is one reason why Jenkerson is now a technical adviser to the Department of Homeland Security and the U.S. Marine Corps.

As the storm of protesters gathered, the St. Louis Fire Department got ready. "The same issues came up, but it looked different than in Ferguson," says Battalion Chief Derrick Phillips, who's the chief of both training and homeland security, and now holds a master's degree in homeland defense and security.

Chief Phillips says that when the fires started in Ferguson, the Ferguson Fire Department was slow to engage. They feared it was too dangerous, as the protesters might throw bricks at the firefighters. And as a result, as Phillips puts it, "shit burned to the fucking ground." So, in 2017, St. Louis did things differently. The department stressed immediate engagement. If a fire started, they would snuff it right away. To do this safely, they used hit-and-run tactics in which the pumpers would roll up to a car fire, directly spray the fire with the water they carried in the tank (each pumper carries five hundred gallons), and never even stop to "make a plug," or open a fire hydrant. This kept firefighters off the street. If necessary a second truck would pull up and do the same, then a third, and so on.

At headquarters, Jenkerson and the other chiefs created a situation room with banks of laptops and monitors to track the movements of the crowds on social media. The chiefs followed hashtags on Twitter, shifting their resources accordingly. Phillips says the plan worked so well that they exported it to other fire departments. They also knew that Anonymous, the hacktivist group, had wormed its way into Ferguson's database and found out where the police officers lived, even digging up pictures of the cops' children. Jenkerson took precautions: he shut down the Wi-Fi access points and beefed up cybersecurity. The department network was never compromised.

They reinforced the walls of headquarters with concrete. They installed guards at the firehouses. They bolstered the manpower by switching from three shifts (A, B, and C) to two shifts—just A and B, splitting up the C shift to boost A and B by 50 percent each. Because cops could be targets of the protesters, and because a fire captain's uniform (short-sleeve white dress shirt) can look like a cop's uniform, they changed their colors to blue.

The fallout of the Stockley protests continues to be debated. The police arrested more than 150 people whom they described as violent; the demonstrators claim that the police used excessive force (tear gas, riot gear). Protesters filed a lawsuit. But one thing is not a matter of debate: the city did not burn. The fire department held.

St. Louis has been at the center—quite literally—of racial tensions since before the Civil War. This is the home of the Missouri Compromise. And the painful history of race in the St. Louis Fire Department, as in so much of the nation, is something that many would like to ignore. The first African American firefighter joined the St. Louis Fire Department in 1921, more than fifty years after the emancipation of slaves. For decades black firefighters were segregated. They weren't allowed to eat in the firehouse kitchen; instead, after they put their lives at risk to battle fires and serve the city, they were forced to eat in the basement. They were banned from the annual picnic. If a black firefighter bucked the odds and was promoted to captain, he would be assigned only black firefighters, thus avoiding the situation of a black man giving orders to a white man. "If you were a black captain, they weren't going to let you command whites," says Battalion Chief Michael Richardson. "That's a big no-no."

Chief Phillips, who's a scholar as well as a firefighter— he studies things like Social Identity Theory and how it can provide a framework to analyze non-state terror organizations—thinks with a wider lens. "St. Louis is a subculture of the greater United States, and that's just how it was at the time." As recently as the 1970s, when African Americans constituted 40 percent of St. Louis's population, only 2 percent of the fire captains were black. Chief Richardson, who is African American (as is Chief Phillips), joined the fire department in 1987. He acknowledges that even though the most explicit forms of racism were banned in the 1980s, "it was tougher, being a black officer."

That was the case nationwide, and some say it still is. "Despite a rich history of black firefighting heroes that goes back to the beginnings of a professionalized service in the early 19th century, firefighting in this country is stained by a tradition of exclusion," wrote Addington Stewart, president of the International Association of Black Professional Firefighters (and a retired St. Louis firefighter), in a 2018 op-ed in the *New York Times*. "Post-segregation, discrimination was reinforced through deep-rooted nepotism and cronyism. For those whose great-grandfather, grandfather and father weren't firefighters—and especially for applicants with the wrong color, gender or sexuality—training and testing became an impermeable barrier." The essay's title: "I Was a Firefighter for 35 Years. Racism Today Is as Bad as Ever."

Reflecting the larger race dynamics in the United States, some firefighters want to gloss over the issue and not even think about color, while others point to structural inequities. In addition to the union that represents all St. Louis firefighters, there is a separate union for African American firefighters, the Firefighters Institute for Racial Equality, or FIRE. Black firefighters in St. Louis can belong to both unions. Some white firefighters bristle at FIRE's very existence, saying, essentially, *Yes, things were bad before, but that stuff's all in the past. Why does black and white matter anymore?*

Chief Richardson counters that, yes, Jim Crow–era laws are gone, but structural and systemic problems remain. "Just because nobody's calling you the N-word, that doesn't mean it's stopped," he says, laughing a bit.

I ask Fire Chief Jenkerson about racism in the service. "I can't say it has been eradicated or erased, but I can say it's not allowed in my department," says Jenkerson. "I work hard in making sure everyone knows my principles." When two firefighters used the N-word on social media, Jenkerson fired them immediately.

The department is 63.0 percent white, 36.4 percent African American, and 0.6 percent Hispanic, compared to the national fire service average of 82 percent white, 9 percent African American, 8 percent Hispanic, and 1 percent Asian. Racial tensions are most likely to flare during times of promotional testing. "I'll tell you what. During times when we're testing, it's a totally different department," says Phillips. "Battle lines get drawn. People start breaking off into their little groups. It gets ugly for a while. Now? Everything is hunky-dory. But as soon as they make that testing announcement . . ."

The St. Louis Fire Department promotional exam has triggered race-related lawsuits for decades. "I'll just put it bluntly," says Phillips. "If white guys do better than black guys, then the black guys are going to sue. If black guys do better than the white guys, the white guys are going to sue. That's just how it goes. It's been that way since I've been on the job."

The testing controversies reached a crescendo in 2004 when the city's first black fire chief, Sherman George, argued that the promotional test was biased against African Americans, and refused to promote the firefighters at the top of the list. The standoff lasted over three years, with the firefighters' promotions in limbo until a court ruled that the tests were not biased. The mayor's office demoted Fire Chief George, who promptly resigned. This racially charged and divisive chapter of the fire department's history happened over a decade ago, but it left a bitter taste that, for many, still lingers.

Firefighters of all races, genders, ages, departments, and backgrounds seem to agree on one thing: the testing system sucks. No one I spoke to likes it. No one. "It's the most brutal thing you ever want to go through," says Jenkerson, noting that the flurry of lawsuits are a nationwide issue; the long list of departments with race-related lawsuits includes New York, Jacksonville, Dallas, and New Haven. Adding to the fire chief's frustration is that even if he had a way to fix the testing, he couldn't; that's all handled by the city's department of personnel.

Chief Richardson has worked at STLFD headquarters for more than twenty years and under four different fire chiefs, which is the equivalent of someone working for the Clinton, Bush, Obama, and Trump administrations. He gives Jenkerson high marks for handling the racial tensions, noting that "he has more black people on his staff than any other chief we've had." Mosby calls him "progressive, for sure."

Richardson holds both views simultaneously: structural racial inequities remain, yet, overall, he loves the fire service.

He loves the work they do for the community. He loves the loyalty among firefighters. He considers the pay fair. And at the end of our conversation he tells me, "We do more good than bad. We cause more smiles than we do frowns."

## Bodies

7:30 P.M.

Back at Ramon's engine house, the call comes just after we finish dinner. Car fire.

Ramon and the guys suit up as they jog to the truck. We slam the doors and Willy pulls us out of the station.

We're at the fire in less than a minute. The car's hood is in flames. Ramon, Tyler, and Captain Duffy leap from the truck, and Tyler, the leadoff man, grabs the one-inch booster hose and charges toward the car. Normally, Ramon, the plug man, would connect the four-inch hose to a hydrant, but for a car fire like this the truck's 400-gallon tank should provide enough water to do the job, and making a plug would only slow things down. This tradeoff—speed versus water supply—is yet another micro-decision that a captain needs to make on the fly.

Tyler blasts the car with the hose. Ramon uses a crowbar to crack open the hood. They snuff the fire in seconds. The two firefighters communicate without saying a word, just nods and eye contact and shared history. They open the car to inspect for interior flames. Tyler coughs from the smoke and it seems like he can barely breathe, but he later tells me it was nothing. Their job is mostly done, but they still need to inspect the trunk to ensure that the flames are vanquished. Ramon tries to pop the trunk with a crowbar. It doesn't budge, so he lugs out the big guns: the forty-eight-pound Jaws of Life, which rips through the car's metal like a stick through tinfoil.

After they finish cleaning their gear and their bodies, Tyler tells me that most car fires, like this one, are pretty straightforward. But not always. Just as with EMS calls, the "routine" can flip to horror. That happened a few years ago when Tyler easily doused a car fire, just like tonight, and then climbed inside to ensure that the fire was extinguished, just like tonight.

Something smelled wrong inside the car. It smelled like barbecue. The smoke in the car began to clear, and on the floorboard, Tyler saw an object that was almost unrecognizable: a human head. Then he saw the body of a young man, maybe nineteen, slumped over the center console. The fire had burned the feet off. The skin was charred. "It looked like a rotisserie chicken," he says to me now, expressionless. "And the smell . . . it was almost semisweet. I couldn't eat barbecue for weeks."

What the recruiting flyers don't emphasize, but maybe should: firefighters need to be able to handle these kinds of shocking visuals, which are included in this book—and on the very first page—as a form of full disclosure. "You're going to encounter sad calls," says Fire Chief Tom Jenkins. "Babies will die. You're not going to save everyone. You have to expect bad stuff, and you have to be able to manage it."

Nearly every firefighter told me the same thing: the hardest part is the kids. "It's seeing their lives snuffed out at age four, or age two, or age ten," says Gary Ludwig, president of the International Association of Fire Chiefs. I can hear the emotion in his voice as he elaborates. "And I know that they'll never date. They'll never go to the prom, or someday take their kids to a baseball game. That's the most difficult part of this job."

Reflecting on his twenty-five-year career in St. Louis, where he was chief paramedic, Gary says he caught three fires where six kids died in each fire. Eighteen kids. He remembers one car accident where a small boy was riding in the back of a hatchback. The hatchback popped open, the boy flew from the car, the boy hit his head on a fire hydrant and was instantly killed. The boy was five years old. The driver of the car was not the boy's parent but the babysitter, so the father had to be called to the scene. "Then the father shows up," Gary says. "I've never seen a man grieve like that." He adds,

"That father never had a chance to play catch with his son. That's the hardest part of this job," he says once more.

Jenkerson tells me about one of his first tough calls, in the 1980s, when he was a new prick. The call came on New Year's Eve. A fire engulfed a two-story building. There weren't many visible flames, just heavy smoke—never a good sign. Jenkerson's company was the second in, so his job was search and rescue. He entered the building with an ax and a flashlight. Black smoke blinded him. He kept low and scrambled to the second floor. With his head scraping the floor, as usual, he could only see the bottom inches of the room. He worried that there were people inside; they might already be dead but he had to find them. As he crawled he swept his ax's handle back and forth across the floor, searching for signs. He found the bedroom.

Then he spotted them: a young couple, a husband and wife. They were lying on the bed. And they were alive. Jenkerson figured they must have passed out before the fire had started; maybe they drank too much champagne. Somehow the fire hadn't yet reached them. They had no apparent injuries. They were alive and sleeping and Jenkerson could still save them.

Then, suddenly, they woke up.

Before Jenkerson could say a word, the husband and wife stood up from the bed and took a gulp of the superheated air. Instantly they collapsed. Jenkerson and another firefighter grabbed the husband and wife, and they carried them outside of the burning house as fast as they could.

The firefighters gave the couple CPR. Nothing. It was too late. They were dead. Jenkerson pauses when he finishes the story. Collects his thoughts. "That one kind of sticks with you."

Richter has stories like this. A couple of years ago, just before Thanksgiving, He caught a fire in the north part of town. His crew had extinguished the flames, but two little girls were missing. Richter's firefighters searched and searched. Smoke still filled the house. "Nobody could find these two little girls," Richter says to me in the darkness of his SUV, his voice grim. This is not a story he likes to tell.

The firefighters searched the bedrooms. They searched the closets. They searched the kitchen. They wore their masks in the smoke and they used their pike poles to sift through the debris. Nothing.

Finally, Richter went inside the house himself without wearing a mask and found the little girls.

"They're right here," he said, pointing just inside the front door.

The little girls were lying on the floor. They were dead. They were in a pose called the "pugilistic attitude," in which the tiny knees and elbows were bent and clenched defensively, like a boxer's, before the flames burned off the skin and the fingertips and the toes. Their hair was gone. "They were a pile of debris," Richter says, his voice empty. Because the girls were lying facedown, their eyes were still in their sockets; Richter knows from experience that if the girls had been lying faceup, the eyeballs would have been gone.

After Richter found the girls, he had to inform the mother that her two daughters were dead. No amount of training, no amount of experience, and no amount of detachment could fully prepare him or anyone for the mother's inconsolable grief. The woman jumped up and down, distraught, screaming, and said she wanted to run inside the burning building and kill herself.

Richter looks at me. This next part especially bothers him: the root cause of the fire. "There were no fucking smoke detectors," he says, anger in his gravelly voice. "We've given out hundreds of thousands of smoke detectors." He pauses and collects himself. "There's no excuse anymore."

## Call After Call After Call

9:00 P.M.

I'm back in the SUV with Richter. After driving around for most of the day to check on his stations and survey broken buildings, finally, at night, we catch a fire. It's a first-alarm fire in the Sixth District. The chief flips on the siren and guns the engine.

Technically speaking, even on the way to a fire, you are supposed to obey the speed limit. Technically speaking, you are supposed to stop at red lights. Technically speaking, you can kiss the chief's ass. He rockets through every red light as if thinking, *What are they going to do, fire me?*

Richter knows that in this case we'll arrive too late to see much. "It should be out by the time we get there," he says, with maybe a note of regret. Technically this is not "his" fire; every first-alarm fire summons is answered by two battalion chiefs—the one in charge of the district and a backup chief from a neighboring district. Richter commands the Fifth District; we're headed to the Sixth as backup.

We cut through a cemetery, and as we speed past the gray tombstones, the chief, while carefully listening to the fire on his earpiece, also manages a dad joke: "People are dying to get in here."

We arrive at the scene and he turns out to be right: the fire is out. About a dozen firefighters emerge from the building, sweaty, their masks hanging off, returning from war.

"It was a good stop," the chief says, nodding. Yet the work is not done. In the parking lot, the ground is covered in hoses and equipment and heavy gear. This is what the local news clips rarely show. Grunting, the firefighters lift the heavy hoses and work together, in three- and four-person teams, to neatly organize the lines in the trucks. It's hard work. It's not glamorous. It takes much longer than putting out the fire itself. The chief sees me watching them. He nods, glad that I get it. "Everything we do is fucking heavy," he says. "The equipment is heavy. The tools are heavy. Water is heavy."

9:40 P.M.

Now it's dark out. With Ramon we catch another EMS call—a possible stroke—so Willy drives us deep into St. Louis's sprawling Forest Park, where we head to an amphitheater called the Muny (the St. Louis Municipal Opera Theatre), the largest and oldest outdoor musical theater in the United States. Tonight there's an under-the-stars performance of *Footloose*. While a crowd of 10,000 people sits on the lawn and watches the show, Ramon and company hustle to a small building behind the stage that appears to be a first aid bunker. Inside the room, a young African American woman lies on a cot and moans in pain.

"*Oh, God, it hurts!*" she howls. She's hyperventilating: big gulps of air, then spasms, then more gulps.

"You're going to be okay," says Tyler.

"*It hurts it hurts it hurts!*" More spasms.

They check her vitals, take her blood pressure.

"*Don't leave me!*"

They use an EKG to ensure that she didn't have a heart attack. She didn't. Ramon tries to soothe her by counting backward, from ten, and asking her to repeat each number.

"Ten . . . ," says Ramon.

"*TENNNN!!!*"

"Nine . . ."

"*NIIIIIINE!*"

"You're doing great," says Ramon, his voice gentle. "Eight . . ."

"*Eight*," with less panic in her voice.

She stops screaming. As she counts down her breathing returns to normal.

"Keep going, keep going, you're doing great. Four . . ."

"Four."

When they reach one, it feels like a shared triumph, and she has recovered from the anxiety attack. The worst is over. As usual, the crew waits for the arrival of the paramedics, who will whisk the woman to the hospital for a thorough evaluation. We leave the amphitheater by walking behind the crowd, in the dark, invisible. These thousands of people enjoying *Footloose*, like most of America on almost every day, are oblivious to the firefighters who are always at the ready, always helping, always serving.

———

10:30 P.M.

Ramon and the crew catch another call, the day's eleventh. I'm exhausted. The firefighters are not. The sirens blare and we speed to the Central West End, the ritzy neighborhood, and arrive at a concert hall where a band called Killswitch Engage is onstage. In the lobby, to the background of death metal, a guy in a sleeveless Guns N' Roses shirt has passed out. Again the firefighters check vitals. Again the patient will be okay.

And then another call, then another call. I'm beginning to lose track. (If I'm a white cloud for Richter, with Ramon I'm a monsoon.) On the way back from call number thirteen, at a red light, a convertible pulls up next to the truck. A young woman is driving. She's attractive. She makes eye contact with Willy, the driver, who's something of a ladies' man. She shouts something from the car.

"I can't hear you!" Willy yells back at her.

"Give me your number!"

He calls out his phone number.

The light turns green. Willy smoothly drives the truck forward, and seconds later his phone rings. It's the girl. He doesn't pick up but he smiles. Ramon and the other guys give him some very envious shit.

"Willy gets a hundred numbers!" Tyler yells from the back.

"Willy's a legend," says Ramon.

The truck fills with laughter.

There are certain fringe benefits to becoming a firefighter.

1:30 A.M.

It's freezing in the bunk room. As one firefighter put it, "We spend all day in the heat, so we want our sleeping quarters to be cool." Like the other firefighters, I sleep in my clothes and keep my shoes next to the bed, ready to hop out within seconds. Sleep doesn't come.

My anxious non-sleep is broken by the alarm. Richter slides down the pole—yes, the pole is an actual thing—and I sprint down the stairs—cowardice is also a thing—and hop into Richter's SUV, where we speed to a commercial fire alarm.

I can barely function but Richter is alert, poised. I ask him how firefighters do this in the middle of the night. "For young people it's nerves," he says. "For old people it's habit."

At the scene the chief sizes up the situation. Cars are parked on a narrow lane in the street—a lane that's a no-parking zone. Richter is pissed. "If this was a real fire, we're fucked," he says, surveying the street, madder than I've seen him all day. His mind is racing for how they would handle it. "Probably a short jack," he says, meaning a way of deploying the hook and ladder in a tight space.

You get the sense that Richter, the man with the Chuck Norris pin, this real-life action hero who has lost count of how many lives he has saved, would rather just pick up a hose himself and charge into a fire. He tells me that the job is less fun as you move up the ranks. It weighs heavier. You can no longer be as cavalier about attacking a fire, because suddenly you're not just risking your own life—you're tossing the dice with the lives of your firefighters. Or, as he puts it, "I'm putting them into fucking harm's way."

And that can be harder here, in St. Louis, in these swaths of broken buildings. The chief has been fighting fires since 1987. He still believes in aggressive, offensive firefighting. He still wants to save lives and save homes. But what if the building is what he calls "bulldozer bait," a hunk of scrap that needs to be demolished? These are the fires he loathes. These are the fires that make him think of the mothers of those firefighters who could die under his watch.

What if his firefighters die trying to save bulldozer bait? he asks rhetorically. "What am I going to tell their moms if they look at that vacant piece-of-shit building? The moms will say, 'Are you kidding me? What's wrong with you?'"

Richter looks at me in the darkness. "And could you blame them?"

We drive back to the engine house. Richter knows that he is the ninth-busiest battalion chief in the nation. He knows his job could be easier. He knows that, if he chooses, he could transfer to a cushier district with fewer bulldozer-bait buildings, fewer heroin overdoses, fewer shootings. But that's not Russ Richter. "I've always wanted to be where shit's happening," he tells me. "And still do."

## The 3:00 a.m. Call

At three in the morning, as always, Jenkerson keeps those two phones and the fire department radio next to his pillow. He thinks about the active fires. He thinks about whether he has enough manpower. He thinks about the shortage of medics. (Months later he would tell me that he has, at last, managed to hire more paramedics, resolving his longstanding dilemma.)

Late at night, with his wife sleeping beside him, he listens to the department radio. He is always listening. As he told me earlier, he can now know, just from the inflection of the captain's voice, if the situation is dire enough to warrant his involvement.

Usually it's not. It's true that every fire is serious, and it's true that every fire is taken seriously, but it's also true that the first-alarm, second-alarm, and third-alarm fires can be handled by the deputy chiefs or battalion chiefs like Richter.

Then there are the big ones. Around twenty times a year, a four- or five-alarm fire will bring Jenkerson speeding to the scene. And on a summer night in 2011 he heard the first alarm, then instantly the second and the third. (A two-alarm fire and above sounds the same as a first-alarm fire, but it rings in every firehouse in the city.) And he could tell from the captain's voice. A fire had erupted in a chemical plant called Chemisphere Corp. The chief hurried out of his home, flipped on his siren, and gunned his vehicle.

As Jenkerson approached the plant from the highway, he could see an orange inferno in the sky. Everything about this felt wrong. Chemisphere bordered a residential neighborhood, which is baffling, given that the plant stored hazardous materials like acid, paint thinners, and highly flammable alcohol. "If they were building it today," he says, "they probably wouldn't be allowed to put it there."

Another problem: the plant abutted Interstate 44, and it's tough to find a water supply on an interstate. When's the last time you saw a fire hydrant on a freeway? And from the freeway he had a bird's-eye view of yet another challenge: the tanks of chemicals were already burning, ten in total, each one loaded with 10,000 gallons of explosive materials.

Jenkerson did a size-up. He thought about how many lines and companies he would need to battle this unholy blaze, and the answer, in effect, was simple: everything. *Okay, this is a new one*, the chief thought. His brain's database lacked this particular file.

Then he learned of an even bigger threat. His deputy chief radioed to tell him there was heavy fire in the chemical plant's yard.

"John, I see it."

"No. The *other* side."

On the other side of the plant, away from the highway, and closer to the suburban homes, were three railroad cars. Chemicals filled the cars. Flammable liquid rolled down the yard—through the flames—and began to heat up the train cars. It was so hot that underneath the cars, the steel tracks curled and buckled. Jenkerson now feared a boiling liquid expanding vapor explosion, or BLEVE, in which a liquid is heated to the point of blowing up. And if those train cars blew, the loss would be more than the plant or a house or even the lives of the firefighters. If those cars blow, says Jenkerson, "we'd lose the neighborhood."

He called for backup from Lambert–St. Louis International Airport—the same airport where he once toiled away as a young captain, pining for action—and used those trucks to spray the fire with foam. The hook and ladders gushed water. He marshaled every resource to set up every possible line. The shoulder of the highway caught on fire. People fled their homes. The police arrived, and they helped coordinate an evacuation of hundreds of residents. The sky burned orange, yellow, and red. Equipment from the plant began to explode. Firefighters hosed down the 10,000-gallon tanks, desperately hoping to lower the temperature. News crews arrived and breathlessly reported.

Balls of flame erupted in the night sky—a fireworks show from hell. Jenkerson knew the biggest threat came from the train cars. Each had a pressure relief valve on the roof. Hot vapors whistled as they left the cars. The hotter the vapors, the louder the whistles. Jenkerson could now hear a loud, terrifying whistle that cut through the night sky "like a teapot times ten thousand." It could blow at any second.

It was time to evacuate. Not just the residents—they were long gone—but the firefighters. They had been attacking the flames with handheld lines. Jenkerson switched strategies. He ordered the heavy hoses to be set up on tripods, which let them blast water even if unmanned—like putting a camera on a tripod and shooting by remote control. Once his firefighters set up the tripods, Jenkerson ordered them to get the hell out of there.

The hoses sprayed the train cars. Theoretically, at this point, everyone could have left the scene. But what if something went wrong? What if the water pressure in the hoses suddenly changed, which would skew the aim?

Someone had to stay behind, just in case, to tweak the tripods if necessary. That someone would be Fire Chief Dennis Jenkerson. Yes, he is a de facto CEO who spends much of his time behind a desk. Yes, he gives a slick TV interview. Yes, he can play, and win, at politics.

But a fire chief is still a firefighter.

Aside from his deputy, he ordered everyone to leave. The whistling grew louder. The train cars got hotter. At any second the train could explode, and Jenkerson was less than one hundred yards away, almost certainly inside the blast radius.

In the glow from the orange sky, the two men looked at each other. Jenkerson says that they both had the same thought: *Are we out of our fucking minds? We're close to getting our pensions!*

The deputy was a large man. Jenkerson turned to him and said, "John, if this thing blows, I'm standing behind you. That way, at least they'll find a little bit of me." Grim chuckles. Gallows humor.

But it didn't blow. The hoses kept blasting water, the train cars cooled, and the neighborhood was saved.

Back in his office, I asked Jenkerson why he stayed behind. Was this about the captain going down with the ship?

He brushed aside that kind of hero talk, as firefighters

usually do. "We were just too old," he said, "and we couldn't run fast enough to get out of there."

It was a good stop.

## The Relief

6:30 A.M.

The firefighters have caught a few hours of sleep. Their incoming shift is good relief—not bum relief, and certainly not shit bum relief—so they'll be able to leave by 7:30 a.m. But most don't leave just yet. They linger at the fire station until 8:00 or later, sipping coffee and bullshitting with their coworkers, their friends, their family.

Then they will take showers, change into civilian clothes, and head straight to their side jobs of cutting grass or roofing a house or working overtime as a paramedic, and then, twenty-four hours from now, they will put on their firefighter uniforms, carefully inspect their SCBAs, check to make sure that they beep, and do it all over again. They will tell crude jokes, they will comfort victims, they will see bodies, they will respond to false alarms, they will train, they will go on yet another medical call, they will save lives, and they will, along with 1.1 million other firefighters, come to our aid when we need it the most.

In the end, how do you know if this job—this calling—

is right for you? Richter considers this question, takes a moment to think. "If you're an ordinary person who wants to take ordinary tools and do extraordinary things, and you don't care who gets the credit or who gets the money," he says in his deep, grizzled voice. "And if you just want to do some good in the world. Then sign up."

*Doing some good in the world*, in all its open-ended possibilities, is precisely the mandate of the fire service. You never know who you will help, how you will serve. All you know is that the call will come. In one of our final conversations, Jenkerson reminds me of something that his father, his firefighting father, used to say to him: "When you're not sure who to call, you call the fire department."

Thank you, firefighters, for answering that call.

## ACKNOWLEDGMENTS

PRIOR TO RESEARCHING THIS book, I had only two brushes with the fire service.

The first came in 2012. At the time I lived in New York City, I commuted by bicycle, and one day, like an idiot, I locked my bike to a rack and somehow lost the key. My bike was stuck. I had no idea who to call or what to do. A friend suggested I call the fire department.

"But it's not a fire."

"They'll know what to do."

"But this is so dumb."

"Trust me. They'll help you."

Feeling like a schmuck, I walked to the nearest fire station—only a few blocks away—and sheepishly explained my predicament. They said no problem. Right away they dispatched a fire truck to rescue my stupid bike, and after I proved it was mine (showing them old photos of me on the bike), they cut the lock. No muss no fuss.

"How much do I owe you?"

"Nothing." The firefighter looked confused, almost offended. "This is our job."

The second time was a little different. One afternoon, also in 2012, I was in my Brooklyn apartment, working from home, and I heard a loud explosion; it sounded like a bomb. The building next to mine had collapsed. I raced outside to see clouds of smoke and a small mountain of debris. The building had been under some kind of gut renovation and a planned demolition had gone sideways, and now a construction worker was trapped under a pile of bricks and wood and metal. He yelled out in pain. This construction worker, a Hispanic man in his forties, was buried beneath the wreckage with only his head and arms showing, like someone sinking into quicksand. Other parts of the building hissed and smoked and looked ready to collapse.

Other neighbors arrived. Someone called 911. Along with a couple of other neighbors, I climbed up onto the pile of wreckage to try and help the guy. We knew we needed to do something, but we didn't know what to do. I sensed a paradox: The guy was trapped underneath the very pile of rubble that we stepped on, so if we moved too close, we risked stepping on a beam or a shard of glass that could jut into him. My attempt to help could paralyze or kill him. So, should we do nothing? Or should we move forward? I felt helpless and clueless and utterly unprepared for an actual life-and-death situation. And just then, as in a superhero movie when you hear the theme music, we heard the sirens of an FDNY fire truck. Thank God. These guys would know what to do.

And they did.

That frightening day back in 2012 when the building collapsed still haunts me at times. Yet for Ramon, Jenkerson, Richter, Mario, Licole, Cody, or any of the 587 St. Louis firefighters, or for any of the 1.1 million firefighters nationwide, the story might not even rise to the level of lunchtime conversation.

I always knew that firefighters are brave. Who *doesn't* know that? Yet, after having the honor to spend a month with the St. Louis Fire Department, I have an added appreciation for their astonishing versatility, smarts, and ability to code-switch. Calling them brave, in a sense, understates what they do. Like doctors they know medicine; like mechanics they know motors; like architects they know buildings. They are Renaissance men and women. And they do it all with humility, grace, and a sense of humor. I'll treasure this experience for the rest of my life. Thank you, St. Louis Fire Department.

Specifically, I owe a world of thanks, of course, to the St. Louis firefighters who so generously gave me all the access a writer could ever want. Thank you for taking the time to patiently walk me through your processes and show me the ropes. The entire department was awesome. Special thanks of course to Fire Chief Dennis Jenkerson, Battalion Chief Russ Richter, Firefighter Ramon Strickland (and all of the great firefighters in Station 30), Battalion Chief Michael Richardson, Captain Garon Mosby, Battalion Chief Derrick Phillips, Captain Mario Montero, Firefighter Licole Mc-Kinney, Firefighter Cody Carpenter, and the St. Louis Fire Department's loyal curator, Mr. Robert Pauly. To the entire St. Louis Fire Department: I can't thank you enough.

To get some broader perspective, I spoke to a wide cast of firefighting experts from outside of St. Louis. Thank you to everyone who helped educate me, especially Chief Gary Ludwig, Chief John Tippett of the National Fallen Firefighters Foundation, Chief Tom Jenkins, Captain Frank Guilo, Chief Billy Goldfeder, Chief Bill Halmich, Captain Angela Hughes, Captain Jason Brezler, Professor Corinne Bendersky, Chief Peter Van Dorpe, Captain Gabriel Angemi of New Jersey's Camden Fire Department, and the editor in chief of FireRescue1.com and FireChief.com, Janelle Foskett, who helped open some very early doors.

This book wouldn't exist without one of my favorite people on the planet and the world's best agent, Rob Weisbach. Thank you, Rob, for connecting me to the Masters at Work series—what a fascinating and worthy concept! I'm honored to be a part of it. It was also an honor and delight to work with my supersmart editor, Stuart Roberts, who gave invaluable direction and focus at just the right times. The entire team at Simon & Schuster has gone above and beyond, including Emily Simonson, designer Lana Roff, production editor Samantha Hoback, production manager Brigid Black, publicist Christine Calella, marketer Stephen Bedford, and of course the inspired publisher who had the idea for this series—Jonathan Karp. Thanks everyone.

Thanks to those who generously read early drafts of the book, including Dolly Chugh, Keith Meatto, Julia Herbst, Chief Gary Ludwig, and Chief Tom Jenkins.

And a special thanks to my mom, who has a lifelong fear of fires, and was an exceptionally good sport during my month with the STLFD. And after finishing this book, I have an even greater appreciation for the sacrifice made every day by the nation's firefighters and first responders. This book was written before COVID-19, and I know your job is now even harder. Thank you, all of you.

# APPENDIX

## ADDITIONAL READING

Bruce Hensler, *Crucible of Fire: Nineteenth-Century Urban Fires and the Making of the Modern Fire Service* (2011)
  A fine primer on the history of the fire service.

Chief Billy Goldfeder, *Pass It On: What We Know . . . What We Want You to Know!* (2014)
  Full of nuggets on firefighting leadership from a collection of fire chiefs.

David Halberstam, *Firehouse* (2002)
  The classic, and heartbreaking, chronicle of an FDNY firehouse on 9/11.

Dennis Smith, *Report from Engine Co. 82* (1999) and *Report from Ground Zero* (2002)
  Smith is as talented a writer as he is an extraordinary firefighter.

## ADDITIONAL RESOURCES

*Firehouse* magazine and Firehouse.com
>A comprehensive resource with breaking news, features, firefighter forums, and training and job info.

International Association of Fire Fighters (IAFF)
>https://www.iaff.org
>The union joined by most career firefighters.
>The site also has a tool that helps show which departments are hiring.

International Association of Fire Chiefs (IAFC)
>https://www.iafc.org
>A national membership for leaders in the fire service, as well as a provider of resources for firefighters of all levels.

U.S. Fire Administration (USFA)
>https://www.usfa.fema.gov
>Holds a vast collection of data on the fire service.

UL Firefighter Safety Research Institute (UL FSRI)
>https://ulfirefightersafety.org
>A storehouse of resources and research on the latest developments in the science of firefighting.

FireRescue1

> https://www.firerescue1.com
> Another site updated daily with news, training resources, and job postings.

Facebook

> Don't laugh. Almost every fire department has a Facebook page, and keeping tabs on these pages can be a good way to learn about upcoming tests and job openings.